Is It Possible to Live This Way?

Is It Possible to Live This Way?

An Unusual Approach to Christian Experience

Volume 1: Faith

LUIGI GIUSSANI

McGill-Queen's University Press
Montreal & Kingston | London | Ithaca

© McGill-Queen's University Press 2008
ISBN 978-0-7735-3403-2 (cloth)
ISBN 978-0-7735-3404-9 (paper)

Legal deposit third quarter 2008
Bibliothèque national du Québec

Printed in Canada on acid-free paper that is 100% ancient forest free
(100% post-consumer recycled), processed chlorine free

Reprinted 2009.

McGill-Queen's University Press acknowledges the support of the
Canada Council for the Arts for our publishing program. We also
acknowledge the financial support of the Government of Canada
through the Book Publishing Industry Development Program
(BPIDP) for our publishing activities.

Library and Archives Canada Cataloguing in Publication

Giussani, Luigi
Is it possible to live this way? : an unusual approach to
Christian experience / Luigi Giussani.

Translation of Si può vivere cosi?
Includes bibliographical references.
Contents: v. 1. Faith.
ISBN 978-0-7735-3403-2 (bnd)
ISBN 978-0-7735-3404-9 (pbk)

1. Faith.   2. Spiritual life – Catholic Church.
3. Christian youth – Religious life.   1. Title.

BX2350.3.M36 2008   234'.23   C2008-900458-2

Set in 11/15 Bembo Pro with Futura
Book design & typesetting by Garet Markvoort, zijn digital

Contents

Note on the Translation

This work was translated piecemeal over a number of years, primarily by Dino Gerard D'Agata, Barbara Gagliotti, and Chris Vath. It was subsequently edited by Michelle Riconscente and John Zucchi. Lesley Andrassy copy-edited the final manuscript.

I have tried to keep the edition as free as possible of editorial notes, but it is useful to point out a few recurring names and an acronym. *Memores Domini* refers to a "private universal ecclesial association" (a juridical designation in Canon Law). Members are lay men and women who dedicate their lives to God. They are also traditionally known as the *Grupppo Adulto* (Adult Group). Communion and Liberation (CL) is a lay movement in the Catholic Church. The author, Luigi Giussani, founded it in 1954, while he was a high school teacher. Originally he called it GS, which stands for *Gioventù Studentesca* (Student Youth). He often refers to CL in the text as "the Movement." For a brief overview of Giussani and his work, the reader might consult John Zucchi, "Luigi Giussani, the Church, and Youth in the 1950s: A

Judgment Born of an Experience," in *Logos* 10:4, 131–50, or
www.clonline.org.

John Zucchi
General Editor, English language edition

By Way of Introduction

This is an unusual book. It is a kind of "novel," as those who first read the proofs noted. In this work the discovery of life as "vocation" comes about not through deduction but through the evidence of an experience lived according to reason, within the same breath as Mystery.

It deals with the path that Father Luigi Giussani took throughout a year in dialogue with about one hundred young people who had decided to commit their lives to Christ through total dedication to the Mystery and to His destiny in history. The Church calls this life "virginity."

Week after week the principal contents of the Christian faith and the reasons that sustained them were approached through a proposal that emerged from the author's experience and from the passionate dynamic of questions and answers that was awakened in these young people. Thus they gradually became aware of their human experience and lived it in a more determined way.

The style of these weekly meetings has been faithfully maintained in the book as a testimony to a particular approach to the great human problem and to the mature conviction and affection that it can lead to.

The book is not meant to be a challenge to common sense or to be presumptuous. It began as a faithful transcription of meetings and dialogues. It is thus a test or, better yet, a witness to a way of conceiving of Christian faith as something interesting, as a destiny for life. It is transcribed word for word, in its material immediacy. In that sense the repetition of ideas and formulae is aimed at filling one's memory in such a way that it might retain something that will be understood over the years and whose reasons will gradually be grasped.

The book can be conceived of as an exemplary narrative where spontaneity, loyalty, and seriousness in the consideration of one's own existence are able to ascribe a suggestiveness to something that most people would censure or disdain because of an abstract fear.

Is It Possible to Live This Way?

1   Faith

1   A WAY OF KNOWING THAT IMPLICATES REASON

If I say, "Is Anna here?" and Carlo tells me, "I saw her back there" – I can't see because I'm short and sitting down – I say: "OK, she's here," and I check her off on my list. Is it reasonable to do that? Yes, because it's right for me to trust Carlo. If it weren't Carlo, but rather an enemy who had burned down my house, stolen my money, spoken badly about me, who hates me, who can't stand me, and he comes and says, "Anna is here," I'd have more doubts about her being here, I can't trust him. I have good reasons to trust Carlo, but this other person, I have no reason to trust him. Trust engenders a knowledge that is mediated, a knowledge that comes through mediation, through a witness.

Direct and Indirect Knowledge

How do you know when something corresponds to your heart? How can you tell? By comparison: you compare the thing with your heart. How do you make this comparison?

What type of action do you have to take? It's a judgment: you recognize that the thing corresponds to your heart, corresponds to your self; you recognize it, it's a recognition.

"This is a stone." This is a recognition that technically is called judgment. It comes as a judgment, has the form of a judgment.

"Anna isn't here." But Carlo tells me, "No, look, I saw her there in the back." "Ah, got it," I reply, "I'll jot it down." This certainty comes about, just as in the case of the stone, it comes about as the recognition of something. I recognize that this thing is good for me. It's recognition.

What do you call that process whereby you know something because someone else tells you?

Nadia and I are schoolmates. Then we finish high school and I go off to my destiny and she goes off to hers. We don't see each other anymore. Years pass, years and years, and then one Sunday night at the airport in Rome, I have to catch a plane to Buenos Aires, and I'm getting on the plane that's coming in from Beirut. I get on the plane and find her in the seat right next to me. "Nadia! Hi, Nadia! What are you doing here? Look what happens in life! Where are you coming from?" "I'm in from Beirut." "Beirut? And what are you doing these days?" "I'm in insurance." "And are you still single?" "No, I have a family. I have six kids." "Wow, you're doing so many things, and how are your kids?" "Great!" "You want a cigarette?" During the conversation she says, "Remember Carlo?" "Yeah, the craziest guy in our class, the one who talked the most, pulled pranks on the teachers, yeah, that nut, who knows where he is. I haven't seen him in twenty years." "Can you believe it, the last time I went to São Paulo – the plane had a stopover there before going to Buenos Aires – I went outside the airport to get a taxi, and he was there hailing a cab. Him, Carlo!" "What happened? Has he gotten his head together?" "Yes, he started a big business. He's gotten himself together (none of us would have bet on that). He became very rich, he trades all over the world. Since then, I see him often because now we take planes together, we coordinate our flights. I take one flight instead of another so I can see him." The plane stops in São Paulo, I say goodbye, Nadia gets off, and I go to Buenos Aires. I land in Buenos Aires and who do I see there? (This wasn't so unexpected. It's someone I happen to see from time to time.) Another friend of ours named Tom – Tom, who's in the Parana tobacco business in Argentina and Brazil, and throughout Europe. He, too, was doing well, things were good; it was a time in which the tobacco business was going great. I see him and I say, "Hi Tom. Listen, do you remember Carlo?" "Of course I remember him!" "Can you believe, he has a family, he started a big business, he trades all over the world ... he's become a big shot! And now he's in great shape, he's gotten his head together." "I'm glad," Tom says, "I would have thought he would have lost his mind, that crazy head of his. I'm really glad. How can I get in touch with him?" "Well, he goes to São Paulo all the time. The centre of his South American business is there. Look in the São Paulo telephone book."

I speak to Tom about Carlo, who is someone I haven't seen in twenty years. I tell him things Nadia told me as if I'd seen Carlo myself, you see? As if I'd seen Carlo, as if I'd followed the details of his life personally.

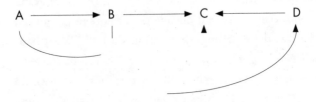

Figure 1.1 Knowledge through a witness

How does this happen? Let's use a drawing to illustrate.

A is me, B is Nadia. Conversing with Nadia who is seated near me on the plane, I learn about Carlo (C). Then, meeting Tom (D), I tell him what Nadia told me as if I'd seen it for myself. I see Nadia, I hear her talk, I know her well, I know that I can trust her. I trust, I know I have to trust. She's not full of baloney, she tells me all the details. Besides, she was my classmate. But I haven't seen Carlo in more than twenty years, yet Tom and I speak about him as if I'd seen him yesterday, as if I'd kept up with him for twenty years, while Nadia's the one who's kept up with him for years. Do you understand? This is a rational, reasonable, indirect relationship.

There's a particular name for something that makes us aware of something else by means of itself: not directly, but through itself. What's it called? Witness. I learn about Carlo through a witness. This happens in two different ways: between A and B the recognition, being direct, is evidence, it's evidence to my eyes, for my awareness; between A and C, the knowledge of C depends completely on B.

Direct and indirect knowledge. The former is also called "direct experience," the latter is an "indirect experience." You come to know something through an intermediary who is called a witness.

Knowledge through Faith

What is this latter type of knowledge called? Faith, it's called faith. What A learns about C, in such a sure way that he even tells D, he learns through B, through a witness. It's an indirect knowledge that is called knowledge by faith. In other words, it's knowledge of an object, of a reality, through a testimony, through a witness who gives testimony.

Is everything clear up to this point? If I see something myself, it's one thing, but how can I be just as sure of what Nadia tells me? If I have adequate reasons for trusting her. If I have adequate reasons for trusting Nadia and I don't trust her, I commit an unreasonable act, that is, one against myself. If I have adequate reasons to trust Nadia, it's reasonable for me to trust her. Therefore, if there are adequate reasons to trust Nadia it's right for me, as a consequence, to accept and recognize what Nadia says. Because if I don't have reasons to distrust Nadia, yet I still distrust her, I'm defying reason.

It's called faith, knowledge by faith, the recognition of a reality through a witness someone gives, someone who, indeed, is called "witness." It's a person. Therefore this is about people. It's a problem that exists only at the level of people. It's a knowledge of reality that comes through the mediation of a trusted person, adequately trustworthy. I don't see the thing myself. I only see the friend who tells me

this thing, and that friend is a trustworthy person. Therefore it's as if I myself have seen what she's told me she's seen.
Did you understand this last part? It's as if I myself have seen
what she's seen. Since I can trust her, since I know I can trust
her, it's as if I've seen for myself what she's told me.

Thus faith, first of all, isn't only applicable to religious
matters but is a natural form of knowledge, a natural form
of indirect knowledge. Of knowledge! If it's indirect knowledge, it leaves the problem of certainty intact. If it's indirect
knowledge, but I can truly trust, I am sure. Just as when my
mother told me, that time I went home, "You know what
happened right here at the corner of General Cantore Street?
A guy on a motorcycle was driving like a maniac. Another
guy came from the other side on a motorcycle, they crashed,
and both of them died." And since I knew one of them, I feel
bad about it; I eat in a hurry, go to school, and tell the guys,
"Be careful when you go out on a motorcycle because one
of my friends just died." I hadn't seen anything. My mother
told me. I had no reason to doubt her story and every reason
to affirm it. I go and tell the other guys as if I'd seen it.

Faith is thus a natural method of knowledge, an indirect
method of knowledge, a knowledge that comes through
the mediation of a witness. This is why it's also called
knowledge through witness. It doesn't necessarily have
to do with religious matters. I'm talking about the same
knowledge that weighs eggs and divides a kilometre into
a thousand equal metres. I'm speaking about the same reason that applies to mathematics, physics ... to everything,
the same reason. Reason has many methods: the reason

that makes me approach something over here, that makes me approach something over there. I change methods, but I know with certainty that a lamppost is over there and I know with certainty that a very dear friend is right here.

Reason is alive. Therefore, it has its method for every object, has a way of its own, develops its dynamic characteristic. It also has a mode for knowing things we don't see directly and that can't be seen directly. You can know them through the witness of others. It's indirect knowledge through mediation.[1]

Fundamental Method for Culture and History

Listen, what's more important: the evidence or this knowledge mediated through a witness? Get rid of this knowledge through mediation and you wipe out all human culture, all of it, because all human culture is based on the fact that one person begins with what another person has discovered and then goes forward from there. If you couldn't reasonably do this, the ultimate representation of reason, which is culture, couldn't exist.

If it weren't for this method, we wouldn't know how to move anymore. Sure, we'd know how to move within a square metre. But with this type of knowledge, we can move all over the world.

Culture, history, and society are based on this type of knowledge called faith, knowledge through faith, indirect knowledge, knowledge of reality through the mediation of a witness.

I don't understand why even society is founded on knowledge through faith.

Listen, how can you trust that the bread you buy hasn't been poisoned, if not because millions of people have always done it? It's all the trust that these people instill in you that makes you go there in peace. If I saw you with a shopping bag in your hand near the bakery, and saw you were nervous and asked you, "Hey, friend, what are you doing?" "I have to go buy bread." "So go on in!" "What if it's poisoned?" I'd say, "Hold on, let me go call an ambulance."

A Decisive Premise

Why have I told you this? Because everything on which we'll deepen our gaze and our affection, everything on which we'll build, is defined through the word faith. It's the sphere of faith, it's reality looked at and tentatively lived in faith. What I'll speak to you about has to do with faith. But our faith, the faith upon which we'll develop all our work, applies the same method I spoke about: knowledge of a reality through mediation. It's a reality that you don't see, but that you know through mediation. But this isn't the only sphere in which the word faith can be applied and used. The word faith indicates a method that reason lives and applies, by nature, in every sphere of life.

We need to use and develop this word faith at a particular level. It's the most important level of all the important levels of life, the greatest level of life. It's the level that has to do with destiny.

If I were to cheat you, I'd be opposing your destiny. If I speak to help you, it's to help you to your destiny. What interests us in the dialogue between us is your destiny, mine, his, hers. Who sees destiny? Who has seen it? Who has ever grabbed an umbrella because it's raining, walked down the sidewalk in a new white overcoat (one of those slick ones), gone thirty-four paces, and happened upon destiny? It can't be found! Destiny can't be seen. Destiny, by its very nature, is Mystery.[2]

Can we say that reason is most exalted in the method of faith?
Perfect! Reason is never so fundamentally, actively, and potently engaged as it is in faith, in the method of faith.

Why? Because A, to entrust himself to B, must engage his entire self, not only a little wheel in his head. When he reasons in mathematics, a little wheel goes round. Here, instead, all the wheels and links and connections with the body and the soul are involved: it's my "I" that trusts Nadia, it's my self. And when I say "I," I mean: reason, eyes, heart, everything.

This is why our friend's observation is very timely: reason is never as exalted as it is in this case. Without a doubt! It's not set aside, it's exalted, it's reason strictly connected to the entire organic reality of the "I." So true is this that if the "I" were, for example, evil, if the "I" were pathological, it would have difficulty trusting and would know far fewer things.

This is the process in which everything about the organism of the "I" collaborates: it's the "I" "engaged with."

This action, by which reason knows why to entrust itself to another, implies a more complete reason, a reason more completely connected with the other aspects of personality. If I go up to someone and say, "You know, I've just seen something beautiful!" and he has a stomach ache, he's holding his stomach, and he goes, "Yes, yes, yes ...," but afterwards, he no longer remembers what I've said because his stomach ache was too bad for him to pay attention to me. He wasn't paying attention, and therefore he didn't understand. To understand, he'd have to not have the stomach ache, he'd have to be working properly, more naturally, more sensitively and be more clearly involved in all his functions. At school, I challenged my pupils by quoting the proverb, "To trust is good, but not to trust is better." There's no proverb more stupid than this one. Listen, if teachers in class are perceptive, intelligent, truly intelligent, they know right away what's going on. They understand right away and know how to come up with the right judgment about student X or any other student much more easily.

People who are most themselves, who have got themselves most together, who are most in possession of themselves, who are most united within the organism of their "I," who are most unified, those for whom everything is in its place, have a much easier time understanding whether or not they can trust someone. Those who, on the other hand, are pathological, who never trust anyone, who are at the point where they can't trust anything anymore, sever themselves from life. The cases can have a million gradations, a million degrees of severity, but they're all the same: these people are cut off from the connections of life.

In faith, reason is engaged much more richly and power-fully than it is in other methods. That's because all the other methods are partial. They have to do with a specific type of object. A man who knows everything about flies and writes a 1,500-page book about them describing every possible quality a fly can have, who's a Nobel prizewinner in science, and who doesn't know a whit about his wife – his kids hate him and he mistreats them – is a pitiful man, not a Nobel prizewinner, because his wife and kids need a reason that is naturally complete and at peace. He is extremely sharp with respect to one aspect of reality, one segment (incidentally, it's a fairly small part of reality), the fly, the phenomenon of the fly. He knows everything about this, but he doesn't know anything about his destiny or other people's situations. He's a poor wretch, even if he is a Nobel prizewinner.

Like that professor of chemistry I'm always talking about who, many years ago, in a discussion among university professors, out of the blue said, "You know, if I didn't have chemistry I'd kill myself." He had a wife and kids: nothing is more inhuman than saying something like this. It couldn't be reasonable; nevertheless he was a great chemist. My mother wasn't a great chemist. She hadn't studied chemistry, but how she treated my father, with all his idiosyncrasies, how she treated us children. My God, how I would like to be like that! She was able to perceive everything going on around her at home. You could see she was intelligent by the way she spoke about what she read in the newspaper.

As an introduction, I've mentioned the most decisive thing. What we'll be discussing will be the content of faith. To speak of Christ, the soul, destiny, the Mystery, is to speak of faith.

The content of all the things we'll discuss cannot be seen. Nevertheless, it can be known through a witness, through witnesses.

Therefore, everything we'll do together during these hours of lessons or discussions rests on reason in its characteristic dynamic, which is called "faith." Everything rests on reason inasmuch as it's capable of faith, faith being the most utmost capacity of reason. "Utmost," because without it man wouldn't exist: history would no longer exist, nor would culture, nor society. Thus, knowledge of destiny would no longer exist.

Have I been clear? We've spoken about this because we will speak at this level. We'll speak, first, of faith as it is normally used, that is to say, the recognition of an invisible content of reality (reality in its invisible aspect). Second, we'll speak about how this content is grasped through reason in its characteristic method, which is called the method of faith, knowledge by means of a witness.

If you reread the first volume of the *School of Community*, you'll rediscover this important observation in the third premise: the more one is moral, the more one is capable of trusting; the less one is moral, the less one is capable of trusting, because immorality is like a schizophrenia or psychic dissociation.[3] So true is this that the most unstable people are the young. Along the way, something gets established in them – since you need to have certainty in life – on a whim, something gets set in them, whatever is easiest gets instilled in them as a path to certainty, whatever seems easiest. And whatever cannot be seen seems equivalent to what doesn't exist. And since what exists, being fleeting, is ephemeral, everything is nothing. Deep down, today this is everyone's philosophy.

An Invitation to Prayer

Therefore I will conclude by saying that we can't begin to discuss these things without some part of our heart praying, asking the Mystery of Being for light, affection, sincerity, and the simplicity to say "yes" to what is true and "no" to what is false.

We need to pray to God to be so truly moral as to say "yes" to what is positive and "no" to what is negative. We need to pray to God, because man is wicked, and, being wicked, he says "no" to the evidence.

You put a glass in front of a naughty child's nose and say, "It's a glass, right? Carlo, say it's a glass. This is a glass, isn't it?" "No!" "Isn't it a glass?" The kid says no, because he's capricious. Men are in the same position in front of life in all its meaning. The word destiny indicates the meaning of life. Actually, the Greek word denotes ultimate meaning, destiny as meaning, *eimarméne*.

I've tried, at least, to tell it like it is. You know what we want to speak about, through what rational instrument we'll speak about it and who I am, meaning I am a witness, a mediator, like all your older friends. The people who are with you because they were put there by those in a position of responsibility are there as if it were me among you. They are witnesses, mediators. By trusting them, you reach the truth, a truth that could not be affirmed otherwise with certainty. If this has to do with destiny, if something we cannot see constitutes destiny and the meaning of life, not reaching it would mean destroying life.

Nothing can be constructed if not on rock, on what is certain. Without certainty nothing gets built. Sure, you could construct a small daily action, but you wouldn't have the gumption to recognize a friendly presence, in another phenomenon, in another action, to whom you can say: "We're in this together, let's get to the next level! Let's go on scaling this mountain. Let's get down to the bottom of things." And you tremble on both legs until – trembling, trembling, trembling – you fall to the ground and *die*. And *die*: later, I hope, but you *die*. Whether it's sooner or later doesn't matter.

Gathering Our Thoughts

No one out there is willing to take the time for silent recollection during the week. The week is the yardstick, the measure, the fundamental measure of man's expression. What is man's expression? Work. Work is the expression of man, since it represents the active relationship between someone who lives, imagines, thinks, feels, and does (according to what he thinks and feels), and reality. Work is the expression through which man uses reality, uses time and space, and creates his life. People will be judged according to what they create. In one week (which is the basic yardstick for work, thus for the expression of the person), they don't set one minute aside to think about their own destiny, about the reason why we work, and, therefore, why we live ("we live" in the most concrete sense of the word, meaning to suffer, to rejoice, to use things, and to create what seems right, what seems most pleasing). So, the word destiny dominates life the way a face dominates the figure of a person. Yet no one thinks about it. On the contrary, our getting together here on Saturdays is the greatest evidence that this destiny – thinking about destiny, reflecting on the destiny of our existence – is important to us. In terms of how we'll treat each other and how you'll treat each other, in terms of the content of this path, with all its speeches and attitudes, we stake everything on fear and trembling before destiny, on the desire for destiny and the longing for a joyful destiny.

When we read daytime prayer,[4] when we read any of the hours from the liturgy, when we pray, when we go to Communion, go to Confession, which should be at least once every fifteen days, let's always remember that what determines that act is passion and concern for our own destiny. Please, see whether there's another aim, another goal, more dignified than this, more human than this, and whether it's human to live without thinking about this.

Many times we have compared it to seeing someone running down the street, in such a way that you notice confusion, a disorientation. You'd tell this person, you'd stop him or her and say, "What are you doing? What are you looking for? Where are you going?" And if he or she were to say, "I don't know!" "But you're running ..." "I'm just running." "But if you were to turn around and change direction?" "I'll turn around ..." this person would be crazy. Indeed, someone who seriously talked that way would not be mentally stable. It would be crazy; it's crazy to live without thinking about your destiny. For animals, it's not crazy because they're not able to do it, but for the animal called man, it's crazy, without reason. The reason for living is destiny.

When reading daytime prayer, reading the hours, or praying in some other way, you have to pay attention, because there's always something, some word or some expression on which your soul can stop to wring out meaning, struck by the meaning of that word. There's a word that strikes you more than the others. You have to be attentive. When you start to say, "O God, come to my aid," after these words, maybe with these very words, when you read — not all of it, you'll be distracted in many ways — you will read, without a doubt, some words that strike you more than others. For example, just now when I was down there following the prayer with you (and think how many thousands of times I've read this psalm), this struck me: "Happy are those who observe His decrees, who seek Him with all their heart."[5] Happy means glad: he lives with a different heart from everyone else. "Who follows His commands." What are His commands? They're the order of reality. Universal gravity is His command. The fact that a plant grows straight, grows in a certain way — because some plants grow crooked — is one of His commands. The word "command" indicates reality as a plan, as order. "Happy are those who are faithful," who adhere to things the way they are, naturally, that is, originally, since they are divinely imposed. Happy are those who seek Your commands with all their heart, this meaning of things, this order of things.

As I have already told you, that professor who said, "If I didn't have chemistry I'd kill myself," was rather tragic, he showed that he was rather tragically limited. Yet it was true that when he studied chemistry, when he dedicated himself to chemistry, he felt most enlivened. One reason why unemployment shouldn't exist is that an unemployed person is really unfortunate, not because of money, but psychologically. That professor of chemistry was right to feel better about existence when he studied chemistry, because chemistry is "His law," and he was seeking the command of God with all his heart. After all, the chemical aspect of reality is part of God's plan and to passionately search for His laws is a beautiful thing. In this sense, all true work is a beautiful thing.

"Happy are those who are faithful to your commands and seek them with all their heart." But "His commands" and "seek with all their heart" are two different things. God, the mystery for whom we're made, is found within the plan for things. If you're faithful to His plan, you'll find something else within it.

Now: "Keep my eyes from seeing what is false / By Your way give me life." "Keep my eyes from seeing what is false," from the fleeting aspect and, therefore, from the deceptiveness of things. In other words, rescue me from the deceptiveness of things. You can look at God's reality in such a way that it doesn't appear in its truth. Therefore, Lord, free me from the deception of things, don't let me look at things with deceit. To say I want something that I desire, and that I won't be happy without it, is a lie, because even if I had that thing I wouldn't be happy. "Lead me in the path of your commands." Make me ever more faithful to things as You made them. Make me pursue and use things according to the plan with which You made them, and then I will be happier.

Our meditations mean to correspond to these two questions which we asked unconsciously during the daytime prayer. Certainly most of us, all of us, asked them unconsciously. Not me – by chance – but all of you did this unconsciously. The meditations we'll have on Saturdays and that you'll have during the week (together with your more mature friends, so that you try to understand them, to study them, and thus to make them yours), are attempts to limit the deceptiveness of our lives, to increase the obedience to God's plan for our life; and therefore, they aim to be an aid in living our lives with gladness, to the greater gladness of our lives. And whether or not following makes us gladder will also be a sign of the rightness of our way of following.

2 THE DYNAMIC OF FAITH

Remember what we spoke about the last time? About method and about faith. Method in what sense? Method means "the way to do something." Faith is a way to knowledge.

What is capable of knowing? My reason. That energy peculiar to man through which he knows is called "reason." So faith is a method of – a way to – reason, one of reason's ways of knowing, or, more succinctly, a method of knowing. What kind of method is it? It's an indirect method of knowing. Why indirect? Because it filters, it's mediated by the fact that reason depends on a witness: reason doesn't see the object directly, immediately. Rather, it comes to know about the object through a witness. We've said this method is the most important of all the methods of reason, much more than evidence based on the senses, and much more than science, which is based on analysis and a dialectic.

The other methods of reason use only a part of man. In contrast, this method of faith uses the whole man. Why? Because you have to trust the witness. To correctly and reasonably trust a person, you need to engage all the loyalty of your person, apply all the acumen of observation, involve a certain dialectic, a sincerity of heart. It takes a love for truth that is stronger than, for example, the antipathy that might arise towards the witness. You have to love the truth. The whole person becomes engaged. Installing electricity in a room doesn't require the engagement of the entire person. This is why faith is a method of knowing that engages the totality of the person in its event. Hence, it's the most dignified, precious method. In fact, if it weren't for the use of this method, society – the development of shared life (*corvivenza*) together as the existence of a society, a small society like the family or society in its totality – couldn't exist.

What is the method of knowledge? Society comes about entirely through the method of faith. If none of us trusted each other, what would happen? In fact, where the naturalness of these things is lacking, people go about with knives and guns. No one can trust anything anymore.

So *corvivenza*, culture (culture is the development of knowledge, but you develop knowledge if, trusting in the discovery that's given you by those who precede you, you add your own discovery, and those who come after you, trusting your discovery, add their own), society (the existence of society), history (the development of society, the changing society) are all based on this method, the method of faith.

What surprised you most last time? To hear faith spoken of not by talking about God, the Blessed Mother, and the saints, but to hear faith spoken of as an aspect of reason, the most important aspect in the use of reason. Why is it most important? Because society, history, culture are all based on it; even more importantly, because such a method implies the engagement of the whole person.

The Credibility of the Witness

You should know all these things already – but you don't – from having studied the *School of Community*, which told you in the first volume when someone can trust another person reasonably. Because you can trust another person unreasonably, which is what usually happens. Many people are reluctant and in crisis in the face of the most correct things, inasmuch as they let themselves be led by the nose, in other words, deceived, by passively trusting whoever guides them in newspapers and on television.

When can you truly trust a witness? This is the only real problem: when can you trust a witness? If faith is knowledge through a witness, if the witness deceives you ... There's a funny example in the text of *School of Community*. Suppose Teresa, who's a very logical and reasonable person, goes walking down the street, and is so preoccupied by her problems at home or with her friends that she doesn't realize a man is approaching her. He's wearing a large-brimmed hat without the thingamabob in the middle. It only has a brim, a larger brim than usual, and half of his face is unshaven, his big coat is full of holes, and his toes are sticking out of his shoes. When he approaches her, he says, "Miss!" "What do you want?" (she thinks he's a beggar who's come for her, for her purse). And the guy says, "No, no. You know what happened?" "No, what happened?" "They killed Clinton." She, who isn't very interested in politics but at least understands that, says: "That's too bad!" but inside she's thinking (and rightly so), "When these things happen it's a sign that something's not right about society and therefore anything can happen." And she tells him, "Thank you for telling me this news. Bye, bye," and she continues along the street thinking, "God, they've killed Clinton. Who could it have been? Someone from Haiti or Santo Domingo, someone from the right, from the left? What will happen now? Will the United States ambassador to Italy, who's an important figure in Italian politics, be on the side of the ones who killed him or on the opposing side? Does whoever killed him love the Church? Will the U.S. keep up diplomatic relations with the Holy See or not?" They're all the questions an intelligent person like her will ask. But she's mistaken. Why? Because she trusted that shady character, that poor guy, that obviously crazy guy she saw for the first time on the street and who told her something that had neither antecedent nor consequences. If she runs to get the evening edition of the paper, the news won't be there. That is to say, you can trust unreasonably or reasonably, in the right way or not in the right way. When is it right to trust a person? When that person really knows what he or she is saying and doesn't want to deceive you. These two categories are as old as scholastic philosophy and make good sense: if I'm sure that the individual knows what he or she is saying and doesn't want to deceive me.

To reach this certainty – if you've studied the *School of Community*, you would remember the third premise, the one that talks about morality.[6] If people are moral, they reach this certainty. If they aren't moral, they don't reach this certainty, or they reach this certainty in an unreasonable way, and trust people they shouldn't trust.

From a rational point of view, it's clear that if you become certain that another person knows what he or she is saying and doesn't want to deceive, then logically you should trust, because if you don't trust you go against yourself, against the judgment you formulated that that person knows what he or she says and doesn't want to deceive you. Trust is a matter of consistency, of consistency with an evidence of reason, an evidence reached directly or through a witness, right away or due to time spent together. For example, say you take a train. You never know who's on the train. There are three people on it in your compartment and you're quiet; attentive to your briefcase and quiet. Then they start to talk and you can tell they're three good people, three regular good guys that you can trust. So you say, "I'm going out for a minute," and leave your package with money in it there. And in fact you come back and find it ... especially since the train didn't stop in the meantime!

We said that the only reason for walking this path is Christ. There wouldn't be any other sufficient reason for the meaning of this path. And Christ is the total object of our faith. How do we come to know Christ in such a way that the sacrifice of our entire lives can be upheld by Him? Even others, those who don't have this vocation, need to face this question because sooner or later they come up against it. Like it or not everyone reaches this point, must get to this point. What good is it if everything goes well but you lose your soul, if you show up with a dirty soul? What did you accomplish? You lost your life.

How do you come to know Christ? Clearly, from our outline of the methods that reason uses, the one that has to be applied here must be faith. We don't know Christ directly. We know Christ neither through evidence nor through the analysis of experience.

a) An encounter

Go and reread the page where the problem "Who is this man?" is posed. He says He's the Messiah: is it true or not? He says He's the saviour of the world, liberator of the world, says He's God: is it true or not? Go reread the first page in which this problem is posed. You should have already read it, many times, especially when you did the second volume of the *School of Community.*[7] But since the *School of Community* was good for almost nothing, because you didn't study it, you didn't understand it, you didn't retain it, you didn't pray to God to make you live it, the *School of Community* from two years ago has gone by the wayside. Thank God that we still have this chance to take it up again.

When was the first time in history, the first moment, in the chronological sense, as in a clock – clocks didn't exist back then, but if they had, they would have marked it – that this problem was posed? It's a passage that speaks about the first two men, young men, into whose hearts a new sensation entered. They heard it from someone who spoke to them. They heard things that belong to the other world. More precisely, they heard those things we mentioned before, which to them weren't strange because these things were common in the history of their people. Their entire people awaited the Messiah, their entire people awaited a liberator, someone who would free the people, the entire people. Therefore, as words go, these weren't strange for their mentality. But to hear them spoken by someone right in front of them, seated in front of them, who invited them to His house ... He invited them because they had asked Him on the street, "Master, where do you live?" because they were following Him with curiosity. John the Baptist had seen a man walk by and, suddenly illuminated by the Spirit – he was a prophet, therefore he had those strange moments – he began to shout, "Behold the Lamb of God! Behold Him who takes away the sins of the world!" All the people who were there didn't take notice because they were used to hearing him burst out with these strange expressions every once in a while. However, two men there saw the man he pointed toward and so they moved, they too moved. They moved and followed, trailed along behind this man. They were two very simple men, the most simple men there. It was the first time they had gone there, so they were the most attentive. They were attentive like children spellbound by a story, their jaws dropped. They trailed along behind and the person they were following felt them trailing Him and turned around. "What do you want?" "Teacher, where do you live?" "Come and see." And so those two spent the whole afternoon with Him, listening to Him speak, seeing Him speak, because they didn't understand anything He said. But the way He said it was so persuasive. It was so evident that this man was telling the truth, that they almost didn't know how to retain those words. They left, and told the first person they saw, "We've found the Messiah." They repeated a word of His whose meaning they didn't understand, but nevertheless, that word was already in people's ears. They repeated His words.

The moment the question "Who is Jesus?" was posed for the first time is the instant in which the problem of faith entered the world. Not faith as a simple method of reason, but as a method of reason applied to something supra-reasonable, beyond reason, unthinkable, inconceivable. Faith as a method of reason applied to something inconceivable, because everything this man said was inconceivable.[8]

The second chapter of John's gospel ends saying, "In front of that miracle, his disciples believed in Him." It was the miracle of changing water into wine. What did they mean? Hadn't they already believed in the preceding chapter? And yet this is the refrain that continues throughout the gospel. When he performs a great miracle, the refrain returns, "His disciples believed in Him." Quite correctly, this repetition is not only not useless but it confirms the truth of what's been said, of what the gospel says, because it's the way that certainty is deepened in us.[9]

A boy goes out with a girl and sees that, more than being pleasing, she is a great person, he can trust her. Then he begins to become her friend because he wants to marry her. But it's with the passing months, the passing years – things aren't always the same, lacking novelty, monotonous – that that feeling of persuasion deepens, until it becomes so clear that he decides to marry her. "We'll get married December 24th." He was convinced from the first moment, but he doesn't say, "We'll get married on December 24th" the first time he's convinced. Going out with her, the impression deepens. He's certain from the beginning, but it's a certainty that becomes ever greater. And when it becomes great, very great, it becomes the basis of his life. It's the same for these people here.

What is the characteristic, then, of this fact? What's the first characteristic of faith in Christ? What is the first characteristic of the faith Andrew and John had in Jesus? They melded their entire lives into Him, and we are here now because they melded their entire lives into Him. We are here because of them. If they hadn't been there, we wouldn't be here. What's the first characteristic? The first characteristic is a fact! What's the first characteristic of knowledge? It's the impact of consciousness with a reality. If it's not reality then it's a dream, it isn't knowledge. Am I clear? It was a fact, a fact that had the appearance of an encounter. The encounter is the form of a certain fact. Eating meatloaf isn't an encounter, but it's a fact. That wasn't eating meatloaf, but an encounter! An encounter is a fact. The first characteristic of Christian faith is that it comes from a fact, a fact that has the form of an encounter.

b) An exceptional presence

What's the second characteristic? The second characteristic is the exceptionality of the fact. John and Andrew watched Him speak for two hours with their jaws dropped. For faith to reach its object, the object has to present itself in an exceptional way. Faith starts from a fact, a fact that ultimately has the form of an encounter. Faith starts from an encounter that's a fact, that's a reality. Reason always starts from the real. The second characteristic is that it's a fact that is not normal, an encounter that is not normal. It's an encounter-encounter, which means it has a characteristic of exceptionality. That's why it's taken into consideration.

Let's say you get on a cable car with a normal conductor and you push your way in and go forward because you like to be in the front of the train. You're up there and you watch the conductor going trac-trac-trac – he uses a crank. You don't go home and tell your wife: "You know what, I had an encounter!" "What encounter?" "With a cable car conductor." But if, instead, while you're there next to the conductor, he stops the train all of a sudden because somebody walked in front of it, and then he opens the window and yells, "Your wife's two-timing you!" And then imagine that the man who crossed in front of the train runs behind it and jumps on at the next stop. He shoves his way on and goes up front to where you and the conductor are. The conductor begins to shake a little and this man asks him, "Excuse me, why did you say that my wife's unfaithful? How did you know that she betrayed me?" And the conductor says, "Excuse me, but I was so scared when you jumped in front of the train that I used that phrase to curse you out – you really should have been more careful." "No, no you're right, my wife *was* unfaithful. You see, I got married. Then I went to England, to London, was there two years working, returned, and my wife had a baby. What would you have done?" The conductor shrugs his shoulders. And the other man says, "And I kept him. Poor kid, it wasn't his mistake, so I kept him. Only the baby grew up and we had to send him to kindergarten, and my wife says: 'Let's send him to the nuns because we'll rest easier with him there.' What would you have done? I told her, 'Send him to the nuns!' And after kindergarten there was elementary school, and my wife told me: 'Let's leave him there with the nuns,' which was expensive, it cost me an arm and a leg, you know how expensive private schools are. I left him there with the nuns. After elementary school, middle school – onward with the nuns, what do you expect? I'm too goodhearted and I left him there with the sisters, paying, paying through the nose! And with my wife who doesn't deserve it. After middle school, my wife persuaded me: 'Let's send him to high school.' What would you have done? I sent him to high school, and a private school at that! So this child cost me! But last week, I had enough! My wife goes: 'Listen, he finished high school with honours. Let's send him to the university.' 'No, no!' I blurted out. That's it, no way! Because the most a little bastard can hope to become is a cable car conductor, at best!!!'" I and the three or four others there listening laugh. Then when I go home I tell my wife: "You know, I had quite an encounter today!" This is right, isn't it? Because it's somewhat exceptional to run into something like that.

The second characteristic of the act of faith is that the fact from which it comes, the encounter that was experienced, is something exceptional. But be careful here. When can you say something is exceptional? I don't know whether this observation is more comical or dramatic – nature, as it is created by God, can be comical, sometimes – because we feel that something is exceptional when it corresponds to the deepest needs for which we live and move.

There are deep needs that give a goal to living, to reasoning, and to moving. When something corresponds to the criteria by which everything is judged and lived, when it corresponds to the criteria with which life is lived, should be lived, when it corresponds to the deepest desires of the heart, when it corresponds to what the *School of Community* calls "elementary experience,"[10] when it corresponds to the deepest needs of the heart, that is, those for which everything is lived and judged, when it corresponds to the most natural and fully present needs of the heart, when it brings to fruition what life has been awaiting, then it's exceptional.

To be exceptional, an encounter must correspond to what you're waiting for. What you're awaiting should be natural, but it's so impossible for what you're awaiting to happen that when it does happen, it's something exceptional. Do you understand me or not?

To find an exceptional person means to find a person who attains a correspondence with what you desire, with the needs for justice, truth, happiness, love ... It should be a natural thing, but it never happens, it's impossible, unimaginable. To be an answer to our heart, to the goal for which we live and judge everything, to the criteria for which we live and judge everything, a person, an encounter, must be exceptional. You can see that, in this sense, exceptional means divine. Divine, because the answer to the heart is God. Something truly exceptional is something divine, there's something divine within it. In fact, if it doesn't really bring you to the divine, it decays.

The second characteristic, then, of Christian faith, of faith in Jesus, is that it comes from an exceptional encounter. It comes from an encounter that corresponds to the criteria by which we live and judge everything, corresponds to the criteria by which we live and judge everything in an inconceivable way, never imagined, never seen, never encountered. I've never had an encounter like that, an encounter like that was impossible.

Listen, the way you read the first chapter of Saint John's gospel is fundamental. For Andrew and John, who sat watching Him speak, it was inconceivable, unimaginable. And after, even everyone else said, "No one has ever spoken like this man." "This man speaks with authority."

I have simply underlined that the exceptional is synonymous with the word divine, with something divine and, therefore, unimagined, unimaginable, never before experienced.

c) Wonder

The third characteristic. The fact from which faith in Christ begins, the encounter from which Andrew and John's faith begins – the encounter gave them an absolutely exceptional impression, therefore the presentiment of some superhuman thing, never imagined, unimaginable – awakened great wonder in them. The third characteristic: wonder. Wonder is always a question, at least a secret one. Wonder is hidden inside a profound question that touches the ultimate fibre of our being. In fact, when they saw Him again two or three months later, that man there ...

After that day, John and Andrew would see Him every so often. They went to Capernaum to go to the market and saw a lot of people standing around listening to Jesus. At noon, He entered a house where they offered Him a meal. The people were at the door, all squeezed in, and He couldn't get away. He was like someone who regretted leaving. While He was there speaking – the Pharisees, the heads of the synagogue, were up front, so they could catch Him making some mistake (after a month or two, they were already worried because people were too interested in Him) – two people arrived with a stretcher on which a poor man lay. He had been paralyzed for twenty years and was all withered, and they asked the crowd to let him pass (as when an ambulance sounds its siren in the street, but the streets are jammed) but the people weren't moving. So they went behind the hut, which, as was often the case with houses there, had a straw and mud roof. They tore away the straw, removed a piece of the roof, and lowered him down.

Jesus turned around – Jesus, the man who gave that impression, for whom they returned home to say, "We've found the Messiah." The oldest of the group of fishermen friends, Nathanael, was prone to skepticism. So Philip, another of them, told him, "Come and see! Come and see Him!" He went to see Him and as he was approaching, that man Jesus of Nazareth said to him, "Here is an Israelite in whom there is no guile." Then Nathanael pulled back, defended himself ("This man wants to deceive me! I've never met him, how can he say that I am great?") "Before Philip called you, when you were under that fig tree, I saw you." "Rabbi, you are the Messiah!" Saint John doesn't even say what happened. It was like something obvious that everybody knew: a prayer, a kind act. The fact is that that man felt he had been seen, when he hadn't even seen him in the distance. "Rabbi, you're the Messiah." That man, Jesus, felt the paralytic bump His shoulder. He turns around and tells him, with a remarkable statement, uniting the physical weakness that the long sickness caused with moral weakness – sickness always brings a moral weakness too, as *The Imitation of Christ* says: "Few people recuperate from sickness," "*pauci ex infirmitate emendatur.*"[11] Well, this is psychological data – and Christ, already so astute, says, as soon as He looks at him, "Have faith, your sins are forgiven." "What?" – think of the Pharisees who are up front, who look at each other without saying anything – "Who can forgive sins but God? He's blaspheming!" And Jesus, who has just said this, turns His face from the man, fixes it on them, and says, "Listen, which is easier, to say, 'Your sins are forgiven,' or to say, 'Get up and walk?' So that you may know that I have authority to forgive sins, I tell you, 'Get up and walk,'" and the man gets up and walks after twenty years.

Imagine those people who are witnesses to these things, who watch these things for one month, two months, every day; for a year, two years, every day.

At a certain point, for example after six or seven months, half a year, they're in a boat with Him at night – go and read this piece in Matthew 8:23–27 – they're in a boat with Him because they got together every so often to fish. A terrible storm comes up; He's so tired that He doesn't even wake up; He's sleeping at the stern of the boat. The boat was already full of water. Water is coming in everywhere, they are about to sink. Then somebody goes to Jesus and says, "Teacher, we're going down. Save us!" And He says, "Why are you afraid, men of little faith. After all I've done, if you're with me why are you still afraid?" And He commands the wind and the sea and it becomes totally calm. Those men – terrified, says the evangelist, scared – say among themselves (imagine how they talk to each other, quietly, out of earshot): "Who on earth is this man?" They, who knew where He came from, knew His mother, were even at the wedding with Him, knew everything, knew well who He was. But His way of doing things, His behaviour, was so exceptional, that His friends couldn't help saying, "Where does He come from? Who is He that the wind and sea obey Him?" Such an exceptionality – because up to a certain point the exceptionality can be explained, it can be a stroke of luck – but at a certain level the exceptionality was such that it dictated to them – those who knew Him, those who could have told you everything about Him because they had accompanied Him for months – this strange question: "Who can He possibly be?" It was inexplicable. It's impossible to conceive of someone who does these kinds of things.

And the same question, two years later, was posed to Him by His adversaries, the Pharisees, "How long are you going to keep us in suspense? Tell us who you are and where you come from." But why would they possibly say this? He's there, His name was written down in Bethlehem in the birth registry! Yet His exceptionality was such that they said, "Tell us who you are and where you come from." They couldn't put up with this outrageousness. The outrageousness of that Presence is unbearable for them, they couldn't tolerate this limitless exceptionality any longer. That is to say, exceptionality is synonymous with the correspondence to what the heart desires and to the criteria by which the heart judges life and all things. Exceptionality is ultimately a synonym of something divine. This is what left an impression on His friends in the boat and this is what terrorized His enemies the Pharisees: an exceptionality that was something divine, and that gave rise to an inevitable wonder.

d) Who is this man?
The fourth factor. Faith begins precisely with this question: "Who is this man?" This poses the problem of faith. The answer to that question is the answer of faith. One person says yes and another says no.

When the Pharisee adversaries told Him, "How long are you going to keep us in suspense? Tell us who are you and where you come from," they posed the problem of faith in that man.

I'm sorry to have gone overtime, therefore I can only mention – and I'll tell you at the next retreat – the passage where the gospel synthesizes all this. When Jesus fed five thousand people, and then they went wild – He hit them right in the pocketbook! – they wanted to make Him king. "This is He who is to come, this is He who should make our life a joy and give us power over the world." So He escapes, flees. And they – the day after, it was the Sabbath – think He's in the synagogue at Capernaum, and, in fact, He was. They go all the way around the edge of the lake to get Him. They find Him in the synagogue and He's saying, "Your fathers ate manna, yet they died. My word is like manna, but he who eats my word will never die." Everyone was a bit vexed at this manner of speaking, but by that time they were somewhat used to it. While He was saying this, the door in the back burst open and all the people who had gone around the lake, those who had gone to look for Him, poured in. They looked for Him for the wrong reason, because they had been fed, but they were looking for Him. Then He is overcome with emotion in front of the people who looked for Him, because He, Jesus, was a man. Ideas came to Him as they come to us, through circumstances, experience. He was moved and suddenly the greatest thing that ever came to Him came into His head. It changed the meaning of the words he was using, "You look for me because I fed you with bread. I will give you my flesh to eat, not my word – as I said before – I will give you my flesh to eat, my blood to drink." Finally, the Pharisees had what they wanted. The intellectuals and journalists had what they wanted. "He's crazy. He's crazy. He's crazy." They spread it around that He's crazy. How can somebody give his flesh to eat? When He said something scandalous, because people didn't understand it, usually He didn't explain, but repeated it. "In truth, in truth I tell you, whoever doesn't eat my flesh and drink my blood will not have life within him." Then the din became a roar, louder and shriller, people saying, "He's crazy, He's crazy," spurred on by the Pharisees. Everyone leaves, so that the synagogue – which was approximately the size of this room, for those who've seen it – empties and His aficionados, the regulars, remain in silence. In the dim light of evening, Jesus is the one who breaks the silence and says, "Do you also want to leave?" He doesn't take back what He said. "Do you also want to leave?" Then Peter – and this point sums up everything (as I said before), this dramatic emergence of the question of Christ and the springing up of faith in the world, this is the moment in which faith in Christ rises up in the world, and it will last until the end of the world – Peter, Simon Peter, with his usual impulsiveness, says, "Master, we don't understand what you say either, but if we go away from you, where will we go? You alone have the words that explain life. It's impossible to find anyone like you. If I don't believe in you, I can't believe my own eyes, I can't believe in anything anymore." It's the great, true, real alternative: either the nothingness in which everything culminates – the nothingness of what you love, of what you esteem, the nothingness of yourself and your friends, the nothingness of sky and earth, the nothingness, everything is nothing because everything will end up in ashes – either this, or that man there is right; He is who He says He is. So Peter says to Him, "Only you, only you explain everything," which means you set everything right again, and you make us see the connection between everything, and you make life great, intense, useful, and you give us a glimpse of its eternity. The Gospel of Saint John, in chapter 6, verses 66–68, truly represents the culmination of the entire dialectic we described earlier.

e) Responsibility before the fact

The last point: The response. What is the supreme characteristic of any truly human act, above all when the human act is in front of its destiny? Remember Péguy: God never obliges anybody. Freedom!

Before all this in which everything is so clear – "If I don't believe in You, I can't believe my own eyes" – this is the substance of Saint Peter's position – before the question "Who is this man?" and before the response Peter gives, one can say yes or no. One can adhere to what Peter says or go away like everyone else.

The only rational thing is the "yes." Why? Because the reality that is proposed corresponds to the nature of our heart more than any of our images. It corresponds to our thirst for happiness, which constitutes the reason for living, the nature of our I, the need for truth and happiness. Indeed, Christ corresponds to this more than does any image we can construct. Think what you want: just show me someone who's better than this man as He's described in the New Testament! Tell me, if you can think of one! You can't; He corresponds to your heart more than anything we can possibly imagine.

The "no" doesn't come from reason, ever; it comes from scandal. Scandal is a Greek word that means "a stone in the street, a hindrance." The obstacle on the road to the truth is a form of falsehood. It's called preconception. One has already formed, already fabricated, his opinion of Him. Christ is to the opposite of what I would like: the political I, I in love, I who thirst for money, I who desire a career, I who want a healthy life. He's the opposite from whatever I place my hope in. And I do so in vain, because nothing hoped for ever comes about. The "no" is born solely of preconception.

I love reading this passage. The piece we'll read to conclude is John 11:45–46: "Jesus, deeply moved by the death of Lazarus, went to the tomb, which was a grotto where a stone had been placed. He said, 'Take away the stone.' Martha, the sister of the dead man, told him, 'Lord, it will give off a horrible stench because he's been in there four days.' Jesus told her, 'Didn't I tell you that if you believed you'd see the glory of God?' So she had them take away the stone. Jesus then lifted his eyes and said, 'Father, I thank you because you have listened to me. I know you always listen to me, but I've said this for the people who are near me, so that they might believe that you have sent me.' And, having said this, He shouted in a loud voice, 'Lazarus, come out!' The dead man came out with his feet and hands bandaged and his face covered in a shroud. Jesus told them, 'Untie him and let him go.' Many of the Jews who came to Mary's, seeing what had happened, believed in Him. But some ran to the Pharisees in Jerusalem and told them what Jesus had done. Then the high priests and Pharisees called the Sanhedrin together and told them, 'What should we do? This man works many wonders. If we let him go on we'll lose our power.'"

Many Jews believed in Him, and some ran to accuse Him. The same exceptional fact, the same exceptional encounter, becomes "yes" in many and becomes "no" in some. There is no reason. They don't say "it's an illusion" – no, no, no, they run and accuse Him. The "no" is always born from a preconception, from the fact that Jesus becomes a scandal, an impediment to what you'd like.

As a fruit of this meditation, pick up the second volume of the *School of Community*, *At the Origin of the Christian Claim*, and read the story of the King of Portugal. It's a symbol of the workings of faith in the human spirit.[12]

Truly, knowledge by faith is the proof of the seriousness and dignity of man. Someone really only says "no" to faith because he is impeded by something he wants, something that he wants that doesn't coincide with the original and deep need of the heart, with elementary experience.

ASSEMBLY

At the assembly, when there is no lesson, what do we have?

> *The assembly.*

Yes, we have the assembly, OK. But what do we do in order to have the assembly?

> *Questions.*

Questions about what? The weather?

> *No!*

Questions about what we said. To ask questions about what we said, the half-baked, neither heartfelt nor remotely serious question won't do. Like a certain classmate of mine, Monsignor Manfredini, the future archbishop of Bologna, who, to prolong classes in the seminary, always raised his hand. He would bring another book – not from school – to read, and many times he would raise his hand while reading that book. The teacher would say, "What do you want?"

without even realizing it! (So we wanted to go to school, because we were wondering, "Let's see what Manfredini is going to do today!") But it was this same classmate who, running to church with me one night because we were late (the stairs were narrow), yanked me by the arm and said, "Listen, the fact that God became man is really something out of this world."

So there he was, someone who joked around a lot at school, saying something like this. He didn't tell me that because he had read the word "incarnate." He said that because he felt something. While he was reading, he understood or felt or said, "I wonder, I wonder how you can understand this?"

So don't ask questions if they don't refer to things that are felt, if they don't openly express feelings that are experienced. This prevents two things: first, it keeps you from thinking you understand when you don't (most people think they know what Christianity is, while they don't, and think they know the Christian lexicon, but they don't). Second, and above all, it keeps you from resorting to abstraction, talking abstractly, which is almost equivalent to talking nonsense – the artifice of abstraction.

There is not a single word that we talk about – precisely because we learned or heard it from Christ, directly or through the Church – that isn't related to what we are living, to life, that is not directed at our heart, the heart, which is the very locus of reason. Reason is inside the heart. Otherwise it's a kite, like Pascoli's kite,[13] that's flying away – but you didn't read "The Kite" by Pascoli, so let's not overdo the analogy.

Nevertheless, these days, they don't make you learn anything by heart. Not learning by memory is a sign that a power wants you to learn by heart what *it* has to say. If, instead, you learn a passage from Leopardi[14] by heart, power can say whatever it wants, but that piece of Leopardi doesn't give you respite, it doesn't let you become a slave of what those on television say. To learn by heart means to make it a part of oneself, part of one's own blood, a great and greatly human experience expressed with a beauty unknown to us. To memorize is to participate in it.

You spoke about the exceptionality of the encounter. How do you go about not confusing the exceptional with the emotional?

In an encounter, what is *exceptional* is the experience of correspondence between what you encounter – the words you hear, the attitude you see – with the needs of your heart. It's a correspondence to the heart that is exceptional in comparison to normal relationships. The more exceptional it is, the more unthinkable it is. It fills you with awe. It is the awe of the truth, *veritatis splendor*, the splendour of the truth, which leaves you awe-filled. So then, what is exceptionality? It's the encounter with something that corresponds to your heart so much that it makes you say, "It's impossible, something impossible happened." For every question that arises in you, you must turn to the first page of Saint John's gospel. You have to imagine John and Andrew with Jesus, who is speaking. And they, seeing Him speak, say "It's impossible for such a man to exist." They didn't say it out loud, but that's how they felt. While they were on their way home, they said to themselves, "It's impossible to find a man like this!" Back there they didn't say it, because they were intent on listening to him.

What is emotion? Emotion is the psychological reaction in front of something you encounter. Emotion is the most sweet, and tender, and surprising sense of panic that John and Andrew felt, but without one thing that the hint of exceptionality has. The experience of exceptionality has something within that emotion does not: a judgment by the mind, a recognition by the mind, a judgment. What is still missing in emotion is the recognition by the head: judgment. Emotion is something that happens to you, that you feel. Exceptionality is something that you feel and judge, something that you think. It is a thought. More precisely, it is a judgment.

What is judgment? It is the comparison between our heart's criteria and the reality that you happen upon. The criteria of the heart are stable principles, principles that allow you to judge what you find and then say, "It's great, it's true." You feel that it's great and that it's true, but you don't judge it yet. It's like a frissonnement, being moved. You hear something that makes you want to cry: that's emotion. Exceptionality, on the other hand, is a judgment. You say, "It doesn't get any better than this. I've never met anything like this." Is that clear?

I still don't fully understand the word "correspondence" as judgment. In particular, these needs aren't so clear in relationships.
The needs are very clear. What's not clear is how you apply them. It's not clear how to apply and use them. To judge,

what do you have to use? The needs you have inside you. If you use something else, you alienate yourself, it becomes alienation. If you use other criteria, they are criteria of the culture that surrounds you, and because of that, you are alienated, you are a slave to other people's criteria.

The criteria are always very clear, and right inside you. They are called "heart": the need for happiness, for truth, for goodness. However you may feel towards those you meet, you have these needs within. You have to apply them.

Does this encounter correspond to my need for happiness, for truth, for beauty, for goodness? There may be a road to travel. You can quickly say "yes" on impulse, in which case emotion tends to become judgment. That's exactly how it is for people these days: emotion is the same as judgment (I like it, I don't like it). And this is man's ruin. It's the primacy, the predominance, of the beast, the animal.

Emotion is a psychological or, better yet, psychic reaction that must be judged. "What a beautiful head of lettuce!" and on the contrary it's a poisonous herb that looks like lettuce. In fact, the city puts up those "Poisonous Grass" signs. If you don't keep an eye out and you aren't careful ... But you're careful when you already know there's something dangerous out there. If you don't know that, you aren't careful. Jesus came precisely to tell us, "Watch out, be on the alert."

Judgment, however, is the application of criteria that you have in your heart to the object that creates an emotion in you. It could be an intense and favourable emotion. For example, you fall in love with a boy or girl. Falling in love with someone is an emotion that you feel. Is it right because you feel it? You feel it, so what do you do? Does the emotion that I may have for this person correspond to the destiny that God gave me or not? Does it correspond to the calling, to the vocation that God gave me or not? And therefore, does it correspond to my path for happiness? The path of happiness is the destiny to which God called you; it is the vocation to which God called you, the task that God entrusted to you.

One time, I said Mass at eleven o'clock in a church in Milan. The mass ends, I go into the sacristy (it was a tiny sacristy because the church had been bombed). In walks a pale woman, with a baby in her arms, who tells me, "Father (I had never seen her before), my husband left this morning." I stopped in my tracks. "What? Why did he leave?" "He left because he fell in love with his secretary." "Why, had you fought?" "No, no, no. He even left home crying, saying, 'I feel terrible about the pain I'm causing you. I'll regret it, but I have to do it. I'm in love!' And he held the baby and kept kissing her." Look how low you can sink! Torn up because he had to leave her, but he had to do it because he was in love. This is the emblem of emotion elevated to judgment. Am I making myself clear? From emotion, he establishes a criterion of action without judgment.

What does judgment mean? You're in love; you're in love with the secretary, as can happen to many people; as happens, especially nowadays, to everyone. Does this correspond to the plan that God has for your life, and therefore to your path to happiness, or not? Let's see: you're married, so married that you have a baby. Therefore, if you abandon your wife and child, you betray the task that God gave you, so you're no longer on the path to happiness. And even though it may seem like happiness to run away with the sec-retary, even though that may seem like a greater happiness, it's the opposite. It will bring you the opposite. You're crazy. The case I just cited is outrageous lunacy, but it illustrates a widespread attitude. This is the kind of motive, concealed to various degrees, behind all the mistakes people make in this world: the un-judged emotion. The road to destiny is not laid out by, and all the less saved by, that poor wretch falling in love with his secretary, but by being faithful to his wife and his child, to the vocation that God had given him. It would have been a very great sacrifice. Think what a sac-rifice it would have been for that man to shut out the need to run away with his secretary to stay with his wife and child. It's a sacrifice to the point of dying – you have to do it to the point of dying, because "what good does it do to get every-thing you want if you lose yourself?"[15] Jesus said.

Judgment means to pay attention to the correspondence with the heart's needs. The needs of our heart, the funda-mental ones, which always remain, indicate the link with destiny, the relationship with destiny, the relationship with God. If you go against these needs, if you go against God's plan, if you go against God's will, if you go against God's law, you go against the heart's needs. That is why no feeling remains human unless it judged. Emotion is a reaction. Cor-respondence is a judgment that compares the emotion that is awakened in us to the needs of the heart that describe the path to destiny. Emotion is judged when it faces a compari-son with heart's needs. The heart's needs express the ultimate criteria to follow, which is the will of the One who made us and who awaits us at the end. The needs of the heart describe the path to destiny. The Gospel says so, "Whoever loves his life will lose it." Whoever is attached to his or her emotion, to his or her way of feeling, will lose himself or herself.

What is meant by "the 'yes' I say to Christ implies the totality of my person?" Because even if the reasonableness of being here is evident to me, I often feel fragmented. My affection finds it hard to adhere.

My house is in a certain city, set on a beautiful hill, in a beautiful place, you can even see the sea, the mountains ... it has everything! I went into exile and must return home. What must I do? A journey: there's a long journey to take before arriving home. So, my friend, to see Christ in everything, you have a long journey to take. Begin. Begin by setting your mind, every morning when you wake up, on thinking about Christ as often as you can throughout the day. But it can't be your intention. It must be your asking: "Lord, come to my mind often today." "Come, Lord Jesus," the Bible says. You get ready to go to school or your office with the desire to think of Him often.

What could it mean to think of Him often? To think of Him: for example, imagining yourself like John and Andrew in front of that man while He's speaking. Or judging what you need to judge – the behaviour of the others – according to the fact that God became presence, is present to you, is present to everyone and no one knows it. And you get a lump in your throat just thinking that no one knows it. In time, this is what makes you mature in everything.

That's the value of the companionship, and particularly the value of those within the companionship who have already walked a stretch of the path. They remind you of it. True friendship reminds you in such a way that it fills your time as much as possible with the thought of the great Presence, of Christ. That's the reason why those who went with Christ got together among themselves. They didn't even know each other, and they became friends. No greater reason than this creates friends. Because if I have a sympathy or preference, this is the very thing that makes it stable for me. The thought of Christ makes it stable for me.

As I always say to college students: my friend, what is the girl you like made of? She's certainly not made of polenta, she's certainly not made of ashes, certainly not made of gold ... God, even if she were platinum! In front of Christ, John and Andrew understood that another world was revealing itself to them, another world! We're living another world (through which we are men) – source of happiness and peace, source of attractiveness and creativity. It's another world. We must climb aboard this other world. God has pushed us to the threshold, pushed us to its border. We have to cross this border and enter. To live is to enter inside this real world. Really, things are a hundred times more beautiful. So, the girl that you like is made of Another, is made up of Christ – "Everything consists in Him" [16] – the mountains, this girl's body, is made up of Another, because by herself, she would be nothing, nothing.

Who made you find her? The Lord of time, who is the master of time, the Lord of history. Who will preserve her for you forever? Who will assure the eternity of the relationship? Either you don't think about it not lasting forever (in which case you're a fool) or you die, suffocate. Because if you are in a loving relationship that you think might end, that end becomes like a wall in front of your nose – it comes closer and closer to your face until it suffocates you. That presence suffocates you, it becomes desperation. And not only does the superficial person, the slob, the one who's distracted (in other words, everyone!) despair ... This is why everyone's greatest necessity is a big hullabaloo, and everyone's greatest horror is silence, because silence brings these things to light.

May it become *habitus*, as Saint Thomas says, habitual, to perceive in all things – in everything, from the boughs of the tree to the hairs of the person you like – the presence of the Mystery that became a man in flesh and blood and therefore the presence of Christ ("I will be with you all days until the end of the world"[17]). Getting used to seeing this in everything is a history that God allowed you to begin. Ask the Blessed Mother to not betray it. Be faithful to this history.

What helps us in this history is asking God, when you wake up, every morning when you wake up. That's why I insist on the Angelus. You must get used to saying the Angelus, because it is a reminder of the moment everything began. It is a recollection of the moment when what is happening in the present moment began. Because man starts from the present. He can't start from the past. If he starts from the present, he will see that the past confirms this present. The past gives reasons for this present, and the strength of this present makes it possible to judge the past. Say the Angelus well. "May it happen to me according to Thy word," in the relationships with all the people at work, in the relationships with all the people you'll see on the subway or on the street, in the relationships with things, with the rain that annoys you, or with the sun that is too hot – you need to ask.

There's human help in this, which is the companionship. But not just any companionship: the companionship of people called to search just as you are searching. And you understand, then you understand, that that companionship is the only truly human, totally human, reality in the world. All the rest of the world is human like a huge wound that cries out to be healed, a great solitude that has to be surprised by an illumination, by a protection that comes from others like yourself. The companion, then, becomes truly another self, and among strangers like us an affection is born, an affection greater than that for your father and mother, right down to emotions. That's because the judgment of correspondence matures until it identifies itself with emotion. There's an emotion before the company that God gave you for the discovered journey, for the journey of the vocation, which attains a deeper emotion than the one you have for your father and mother (as the holy gospel says). It's not so that you forget your father and mother, but so that you learn to understand that the importance of your father and mother is that they have, in some way, collaborated on this path (for example, by giving birth to you), so that if they were (pardon the suggestion), if they were both idiots, you would love them as you love your companions. Next!

The recognition of this correspondence isn't always immediate. It often demands an effort and a sacrifice from me. For example, at work, even recognizing that I have to work less to give more room to

Christ requires a sacrifice. I wanted to know if it's right to feel this effort.

The recognition is always a comfort, like exiting from a dark tunnel into the sunlight: it's always light, it's always joy, it's always certainty. Given the way your life and the life of the world are set up, applying this recognition becomes an effort, an unavoidable sacrifice.

Take heed! The application of this judgment of correspondence, the application of the memory of Christ, must never coincide with diminishing your duty. It can't coincide, for example, with an unpredictable, disloyal, disordered decrease in your work. You must do all of your work. It's something that penetrates the way you work, while you work. With the passing of time, it will become second nature. Picking up the glass to drink, I see out of the corner of my eye that Carlo's imposingly off to my right. That's the same way Christ becomes a Presence, just out of the corner of my eye, a continual presence – but in time. My friends, we're starting off. What makes it reasonable to begin? The search for the correspondence to the heart's needs (and almost no philosophy, no proposal of life, no emotion about life starts by accounting for the heart's needs. Yet this is the most substantial thing for reason).

Either the correspondence to the heart's needs challenges totality or it isn't correspondence. It must be a total correspondence. That is why a path is established, but it is only by beginning that you will discover the principle. No one will remind you of it – no one. Only your mother and your father have it inside of them – without being aware of it, without even thinking about it. They carry within the passion for the destiny of the baby to whom they gave life. They're not even aware of it, but they have it inside themselves. This is so true that if their son or daughter were to decide on a path that is contrary to what they foresaw, they would concede only in the face of one thing: the child's happiness. So true is it that if they see that their child is happy, first they resist, resist, resist, and then, eventually, they give in. There'll be a great celebration when they give in! But they *will* give in, everyone gives in when they see their child cheerful, because it's impossible to spend ten years disapproving of a situation in which your child is cheerful. Impossible.

The awe, the profound question which is the third characteristic of faith, struck me a lot. I want to understand it better because I always thought that the question started from me. Instead, the awe comes even before the question.

Certainly! You can't ask a question if it doesn't attract you. Something attracts you, so you incline yourself toward it. To incline yourself means to ask. So, to incline yourself toward something, something must incline itself toward you. You must be attracted. To reach out toward, you must be attracted. Once you're attracted, you ask.

John and Andrew didn't know Him, never saw Him before. They follow behind Him timidly and stay there all afternoon *to see* Him speak, because they didn't really even understand what He said. It was so evident that that man said true things, even if they didn't understand them, that after they left, they repeated to others what He had said as if they were their thoughts. Always go back to those pages: as they saw that man speak – and the more He spoke, the more this occurred – the desire in John and Andrew to know Him, to stay with Him, to hear Him speak again, was natural. And this desire was a question, it was like a question; it made them ask the question, "May we stay with you. Keep talking, speak to us forever." It was really like this, because one day, in the synagogue in Capernaum, Simon said it clearly with that sentence that will remain for all of history: "If we leave you, where would we go? You alone have words that explain life."

The characteristics that define faith can be used also for the encounter. I'd like to understand the link between these two things better.

The characteristics by which faith reveals itself are the characteristics you come up against in an encounter. An encounter is the tool, the phenomenon by which you approach faith. Because of this, when you go to church and hear us priests preach for an hour, an hour and a half, speaking nonstop, you leave resenting the faith, not being attracted to it. However, it's an encounter – and therefore a presence, here's where the encounter comes in – it's an encounter that makes you understand the terms of suggestiveness and persuasiveness, of rational truth, of the affective truth, that faith has.

We have to be as clear as possible about these things. Faith is not, *per se*, an encounter. Faith is recognizing that God made flesh is present in the world, in the history of the world. In other words, God made flesh is established as a factor of the world, a factor of history, a factor of present history.

This is faith. When Jesus told the father of the epileptic boy, "If you believe, your son can be saved," the father replied with the most beautiful sentence possible: "I believe, Lord. Help my unbelief,"[18] affirming at the same time both his will to believe, the evidence that there was reason to believe, and the humility of his weakness. And Jesus, faced with these things, was disarmed!

The most beautiful page of the gospel is a prayer by Jesus. It's the eleventh chapter of Saint Matthew, when He says, "I thank you, Father, because you have hidden these things from those who think they are intelligent, and you have revealed them to the simple. Yes, Father, because you have graciously willed it so."[19] To the simple, you can reveal yourself. To someone full of logical reasons and intellectual criteria, you can't reveal yourself simply, because he'll say: "But, let's see, if, but, who knows, it depends ..."

This is faith. How does faith come about naturally? Faith is a human act, therefore it must come about in a human way. It wouldn't be human if it came about without reason. It would be unreasonable, that is, inhuman. The way faith comes about reasonably – bringing within it the evidence of its make-up, the evidence of its reason for the person, any person – is an encounter. It's the happening of an encounter, an encounter between the awareness (intelligence, sensibility, and affectivity) of a person and a human, exceptional Presence.

Now, I have attempted to distinguish the meaning of faith – to recognize the Presence of something else in the experience of human history, to recognize a factor that is more than human, that therefore presents itself as exceptional – from how it comes about. Faith springs up and is attested to humanly and reasonably – therefore in an affec-

tively perceptible and livable way, creatively – solely as the
fruit of an encounter. In this encounter, the great Presence
makes itself evident as the source of an exceptionality, of
an effective greatness that we could never have suspected.
In the very same way, people say what the apostles said, "If
we don't believe in this man, we can't believe even our own
eyes."

In any case, you have to read and re-read these things.
You need to speak and speak about them ten times, a hundred times. Then, you'll become a *mens*, meaning the measure of everything, a mentality, a filter of the measurement
of everything. Those words become a mentality.

Look, the work we're doing when we get together is just
the initial notation of something that must become clear to
you: *you* have to retrace the path, you must understand the
links, go back over the relationships between one word and
another so that they become clear. Otherwise, the real person
in you won't emerge. The real man or woman is free from
the alienation of this world, from the slavery of the common
mentality. The opposite of this is the common mentality,
it's what you've lived thus far, what you're tempted to live
every day. But the Angelus that you'll say every morning
will act like a sword thrust into a crack in the rock, the crack
in the wall of the common mentality. Every day, that space
will widen. You have to go back over these things, understand the links, and then, above all, the whole logic of the
lessons with their five fundamental passages is right there in
front of you.

2 Freedom

THE FIVE PASSAGES OF FAITH

Now, what are the five points we've used to describe faith?

First, an event happens and has the form of an encounter. The shock you get makes you discover something new. It isn't the fruit of reason, it isn't the fruit of an itinerary. It's the fruit of an encounter, of a moment that strikes you. One of Tom's students was hanging out with us in CL for a while. He was invited to the wedding of someone in the community in Bologna. He left the church telling Tom, "Do you realize I feel at home for the first time?" "At home?" "I feel at home for the first time! I understood why my classmate is wrong: because he presumes"– and he was speaking of the most intelligent guy in the class –"to discover things through his powers of reasoning; he thinks he can reason his way to the truth. But instead, truth is discovered, by surprise, in one moment, in a determined moment." This is exactly what we say.

John and Andrew: they lived their whole lives as good Jews who meditated on the prophets, with all the shortcomings and merits of good Jews. They saw that man and, because of John the Baptist's indication, followed Him. When He began to speak, *as* He spoke (and even more so the more He spoke), they were terrified: terrified in the sense of being bowled over, bowled over in the sense of won over. The most beautiful thing in the world is to be won over by these encounters.

But it's exactly the same with the most beautiful aspect of the human condition, with what little beauty there is in the human condition: the realization of having done something good (to have saved a life, for example) – or coming across someone who makes you feel loved. It is something you become aware of. Because we can't understand and follow Christ if we too don't pass through all these human feelings. Only by following Christ do these feelings become a hundred times greater, truer; nothing is left out, everything becomes more true. Truer in awareness of the origin, truer in awareness of the present, the aim of the present, and truer with respect to awareness of destiny.

Second is the exceptionality of this encounter. What does exceptionality mean? Something exceptional is something that corresponds to the heart. Strangely enough, you never find something that corresponds to the heart. When you do find it, it's a sign of great exceptionality. So far, it's not as though anyone would have set forth the judgment: "So he's God." No, no way! We're describing what John and Andrew felt, which they even felt in terms of judgment.

Third, this exceptionality creates wonder. Wonder always brings a secret question with it: how can it be like this? Who is this man? How can this happen? And this is the fourth point.

Fifth: at this point, it starts to become your responsibility to act. Up to now, you've been graced, it's grace. At this point, your responsibility begins; you're the one who has to start bowing your head, you're the one who has to start acting. You, what is the *human you* that acts? It's freedom. We've seen that incredible page where, when Jesus performed His greatest miracle (what more do you want than this?), many said: "It's true!" and others went off to accuse him.[1]

To adhere, you just have to be sincere, to affirm the correspondence; and thus, to be reasonable. Reasonableness means to affirm the correspondence between what you've stumbled upon and yourself and your own heart. To deny this, you'd have to have a preconception. You'd need to be attached to something you want to defend. If you have something to defend in front of the evidence and the truth, you no longer see the evidence, you no longer see the truth. You're relentlessly worried about saving what you want to save. For example, one of the scientists who turned the course of human history upside down, Pasteur, who discovered microbes (the most revolutionary discovery in the history of medicine), was held hostage to the point of them wanting to put him in a mental institution (today they would have killed him). By whom? By scientists from the Academy of Sciences of Paris, who in and of themselves should have understood more easily than others the evidence of his discoveries. Yet, my dear friends, if his discoveries were true, my teaching post, my monthly paycheck, my fame – goodbye everything! The next day I would have had to enter the classroom and say: "What I've told you up to now is bull!" It would be humiliating. So, to escape this humiliation, those scientists were the last to give in, because they were attached to something that came before, attached to a preconception.[2] I used a word that works for everything, the word "scandal," which comes from the Greek word *scandalon* which means "hindrance" – like a boulder on a mountain that falls in your path: you need to run to town to get a crane, if you can. Scandal is the objection that comes from an interest that is not professed in the name of truth, in search of the truth.

1   WHAT IS FREEDOM?

Now, we need to become well aware of what we've called the intervening of man, your intervening, that is, the intervention of your freedom. We need to know well what freedom means. The essence of the human "I" is freedom, freedom that implies mind and heart, intelligence, and force of will, energy of will. The only way we can know how to use freedom is by understanding what it is.

So then, where does our trouble lie in having a clear idea of certain words that are fundamental for life? The words that define man, precisely the words that define man in comparison to animals, are hard for us to understand. Why? Because we're alienated by the common mentality. Normally the word freedom means doing whatever we feel like doing. And that's right, as I'll show you later! But not as everyone thinks, because everyone uses "freedom equals doing whatever you feel like" superficially.

But what does doing whatever you feel like mean? There's only one drawback to following Christ, to being Christian, to being in the Church. The drawback is that you are obliged to make yourself aware of all you do. In other words, the drawback is having to be intelligent. Not intelligent in the sense of studies, but intelligent as in the use of intelligence that, deep down, is in the sentence Christ always repeated: "Be vigilant, stay on the alert."[3]

Everyone goes around with a bag over his or her head and just repeats. Yesterday we were going somewhere in the car and there, in the middle of the street, was this kid on a bicycle who had his tongue sticking out to here, singing "Oooooh!" – a troglodyte. Most kids are like that on the inside. Even if they aren't just like this materially (many are like this materially – more and more), on the inside they go "Oooooh!" They repeat the songs they hear or, worse still, just bob their heads back and forth. In other words, it's the most mechanical reduction possible of what they hear; they don't even repeat what they hear.

The Experience of Satisfaction

What must we do to understand the words that have to do with our life? For example the word justice, the word love, the word happiness, the word life, the word freedom – to understand what freedom is, what do we have to do? We have to begin from the experience that makes us feel free. There's a particular experience in which one feels free, and there's one in which one feels *not* free.[4] When do you feel free? When a desire is satisfied.

Let's suppose someone from *Memores Domini* wanted to go to the Caribbean (nine days with Club Med in the Caribbean), so he asks Carlo: "Can I go to the Caribbean for nine days? My aunt's giving me a thousand and *Memores Domini* can give me the rest!" Carlo, very gently (as he always is when he crushes someone), gently crushing him, says: "No." I swear this guy would feel denied, suffocated, mortified, like a slave, he wouldn't feel free. But if Carlo, in a moment of madness, were to tell him: "Yes, yes, go!" "Ahhh": he would feel free.

Beginning from experience – here's the catch: remember that man can only start from the present, because the previous minute no longer exists, and the next minute is not here yet. We always begin from the present, from the present as experience. Otherwise it's a false present, it's an abstraction.[5] You always start from the present; this is why Christ wanted to be present throughout all of history. And to get to Christ, you have to start from the present, you have to discover Christ as a presence. You understand who He is afterward, and then you also understand who He was two thousand years ago. Our experience tells us that we feel a sense of relief and of freedom when a desire of ours is satisfied, and it tells us that when a desire of ours isn't satisfied (when we're told "no"), there's at least an instant of negative repression, like a kind of slavery.

All those who move out of their homes do so for this reason. And all those who, staying home, return home at night without much enthusiasm (and almost everyone understands this) are that way for this reason: they feel repressed in their desires.

Now, what do you gather from this observation? That from experience (because man starts from experience, what starts from experience is true, so much so that God wanted to communicate Himself to man through carnal experience, in time and in space), from experience, we are told that freedom indicates a moment of oneself, an awareness of oneself in which the relief granted by a satisfied desire predominates. Freedom equals satisfaction, *satisfacere* (to satisfy), the satisfied desire. Instead of satisfaction, you could use the more metaphysical word: perfection. Freedom is perfection. In Latin, *perficere* (to fulfill) means the very same thing as *satisfacere* – a satisfied desire is a fulfilled, perfected desire.

I want to go to the Caribbean, and Carlo says yes and I, all content, happy and free, tell others. I communicate this news to others: "I'm leaving the day after tomorrow." I go to the Caribbean, then I return with a long face, worse than before. "What? Didn't you go to the Caribbean?" "Uh, I don't know."

If this satisfaction, this perfection, isn't total, if it isn't totalizing, if it has some hole that water leaks out from, if it has a crack of some sort, if something is left open, there's no freedom. It's sadness, the hole is the sadness. As Dante said: "Everyone vaguely pictures in his mind/ A good the heart may rest on, and is driven/ By his desire to seek it and to find."[6] That's how the heart of man is made. "Everyone vaguely pictures in his mind /A good [perceives the existence of a good, this is happiness, satisfaction] the heart may rest on and is driven/ By his desire to seek" [*seek*, man's seeking is always a question]; wherefore each one strives to attain [*to attain*, in other words, to join, is *joindre* in French; he *strives*,

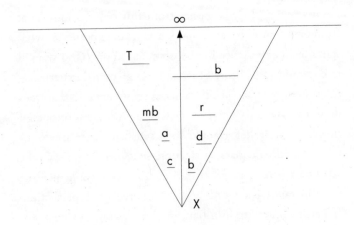

Figure 2.1   The trajectory of man towards his fulfillment

his whole self is striving for, *con-tende* with all the factors of his life, and to strive for implies the circle of human friendship and company, too; his whole self is striving towards attaining this good]."

The Trajectory of Freedom

Let's use a drawing to help us understand (Fig. 2.1): *X* is the point where man starts, existence begins here.

Man has a dynamic that never lets him rest, there is never one moment equal to another: the man who stops is ruined (that is, dead!).

Let's describe man with an open angle: the dynamism of man stretches always farther ahead, always more towards satisfying himself, always more towards fulfilling the desires he has within. Now the ultimate definition of the word freedom – if freedom is satisfaction and perfection – is, as Dante said, "a good the heart may rest on," the good in which everything gets resolved. This good in which everything gets resolved is infinite because no matter what a man has, he still says, "And afterwards?" Whatever he reaches, he says, "And then?" Whatever he enjoys ...

"What I grasped most covetously in my clenched fist came apart like the rose under the vault of eternity ... the more so for what I most treasured."[7] The more one loves, the more he needs Christ, because Christ saves what man loves, forever. At least from this point of view, we have to accept Him. Either we love nothing or, the more we love, the more Christ is necessary to safeguard what we love, to maintain what we love, otherwise we lose it. The day after tomorrow it's gone.

The "I" is relationship with the infinite (the ∞ sign in the figure). The whole dynamic, the whole dynamism of the "I" develops and tends towards perfection, that is, fulfillment of yourself that cannot be found no matter what point you reach, as I have already said in *The Religious Sense*. And, in fact, the heart is the need for truth, justice, happiness, and this can never be found in anything man reaches. Therefore, what man is tensed towards approaches something beyond, always beyond: it's transcendent. This is how the awareness of the self perceives the existence of something *else*, that is, of God, of the Mystery, God as Mystery. For now, we'll indicate it like this: God (∞) is the extreme limit towards which the desire of man is tensed. The closer to ∞ one gets, the greater the freedom. Actually, freedom is the relationship with ∞, freedom will be realized, it isn't realized yet. Freedom will be realized when man is happy. If freedom is the desire for happiness, the event of freedom will be reached when the desire for happiness is satisfied. Freedom – as all Saint Thomas's philosophy says, and all the Church's thinking says, and as Jesus says in the gospel – is the relationship with the infinite, with God. It is the realized relationship with the Mystery. Freedom is the capacity to reach destiny. Freedom is the link, the relationship with ultimate destiny. It's the capacity to reach God, in the sense of ultimate destiny. We live freedom as a capacity for something that has to come at the end.

The space defined by this angle is man's life, in a freedom still isn't complete, in *b* it's not complete, in *c* it's not complete, in *d* it's not complete. It will only be complete here (∞). Incomplete, that is, imperfect: we live freedom at an imperfect level.

If freedom is the experience of satisfaction, of completeness, then this completeness, this satisfaction, in its total acceptance, comes about in relationship with the Mystery, with the infinite; before totally realizing the relationship with the infinite, freedom is something incomplete, unfulfilled, something not yet actuated, that is being activated. Life, therefore, is the road of freedom actuating itself, realizing itself, but it's an imperfect freedom.

2   HOW FREEDOM MOVES

Now there are two fundamental ideas.

a) Through creatures.

First of all, how does this dynamic of freedom within this
X here move? If freedom is a relationship with the infinite,
how does it move? The infinite has to reach it to solicit it,
as you have to do with someone who's sleeping, you have
to call him. What does the infinite do to call me, to appeal
to my freedom? How is freedom activated? Enzymes move
in response to hunger. The stimulus provokes them. How
does God become a stimulus such that man moves? Through
creatures. Creatures are the way the infinite becomes present
to man's heart and awakens a thirst for itself. The infinite
awakens a thirst, awakens the needs for happiness, justice,
truth, love. The needs for justice, truth, love are set in motion
through the stimulus that comes from creatures [Giussani is
using creatures in the theological sense: created beings, exis-
tence], which are the little bits of time and space, that little
piece of something $(a, b, c, d ...)$ through which the infinite
Mystery touches you, because all things are a sign of God.
For example, this point stands for a mountain, Mont Blanc
(mb) and man – the diagram should have another dimension, but never mind – upon seeing Mont Blanc, says: "How
beautiful! Would that I could have a relationship with what
made this thing! Oh that I could embrace Mont Blanc!" And
then the little boy grows up, and after having seen Mont
Blanc, sees *the* "white mountain": a girl (r). The girl attracts
him more than Mont Blanc!

Therefore, first: freedom enters into action, the dynamic
of freedom enters into action because it's touched by creatures (he's touched more or less according to how much the

creature corresponds to him), following how God appears to him, and He appears to him in things as signs.

To be sure, there's a condition: you need to be attentive, sincere. Do you know why Jesus said: "Blessed are the poor?" Do you understand why Jesus loves children and makes them a sign? You need to be free of preconceptions. You need to face things and feel the pure and original reminder in them: "I thank you, Father, because you have revealed them not to those who think they are, but to the simple."[8] The simple are those who call a spade a spade, who tell it like it is.

What's the opposite of this? It's falsehood, falsehood is counter to freedom: the opposite of freedom is falsehood. In fact, in John's gospel, sin, which is the opposite of freedom, is identified with falsehood. Sin is a lie. What is the truth of this r? Its relationship with the infinite; r is a morsel that represents the infinite for me. This r is a morsel that represents the infinite more than this mb does.

b) Imperfect freedom.

Now, what happens? Let's suppose freedom is a steam engine, a horse, an airplane ... let it be some means of transportation. It arrives here and says: "How beautiful!" It halts to praise God because it sees Mont Blanc. It arrives at this point (r), it feels attracted by this point here. The person I'm talking about (X), is a doctor in Tanganyika [the former name of the African country, Tanzania] because the idea of mission in Tanganyika attracted him; he made vows dedicating his life to this work, he became a friar in order to go to Tanganyika. Here, you need to put your imagination to work a little more. As a friar in Tanganyika (T), he meets a blonde (b), got it? Therefore we need two layers: as if T and b occurred simultaneously. While he's in Tanganyika working as a friar (having already made final vows), he meets this blonde and says: "The blonde attracts me more than being a friar. So, if the blonde satisfies me more, I have a right to go off with the blonde." Like the husband of that woman (poor thing!). If he was more attracted to the secretary, why *shouldn't* he have gone off with the secretary? Because in the plan of life, the mystery of God asked this task of him, gave him this vocation, even if it made him meet the other woman. What's the fundamental law? The fundamental law is that he reach out for here (∞): that he reach out towards his destiny. If the law is to reach for destiny (∞), T is closer, it would bring him closer than b, it would allow him to walk farther. Is this clear? But this b attracts him more. T corresponds more to the needs of his heart, despite what it seems, because the need of the heart is total happiness, is destiny. But the greater emotion is here at b, so he gives in to the emotion and veers off here. Clearly he strays from the path. This is the concept of sin. In the dynamic of freedom the possibility of sin – which is choosing, in the face of a creature, what is immediately more satisfying, instead of using the creature to extend further towards the destiny we're made for – is implicit. Sin is leaving, getting off the path to destiny to linger over something that interests us more in the moment. It isn't clear? Well, you'll think it over.

Why can freedom make this mistake? If one were to reflect, if one were like Socrates or like Seneca, like a great Stoic or a great philosopher, would one not commit this error? No! Even they made this mistake. Everyone makes mistakes. Everyone commits in one way or another. Why is freedom like this? Because it is not yet complete. Only when it gets here (∞), freedom, upon finding itself in front of its complete object, will be able to choose no longer, but will be completely full, will be completely satisfied. It won't be able to have the temptation to choose something else. Now then, I've already said the second important thing: since it is on the way towards destiny, imperfect freedom can make mistakes. To sin means to come up short, *amartànein*, to come up short on a journey and to take another road (for example, in the desert, if the caravan loses its compass, it goes off in the wrong direction).

Freedom is imperfect, and precisely because it's imperfect it can choose something that isn't right. The capacity to choose is specifically up to a freedom that is on a journey, not to a fulfilled freedom. Choice is not relevant to the definition of freedom: freedom is total satisfaction. Error, the possibility of error, pertains to a freedom that still isn't free, that still isn't freedom, that hasn't yet reached total satisfaction. This is why it's called defective. Defective: flawed. *Deficere* in Latin means to come up short – for example, when someone collapses from a sudden, serious bout of hypoglycemia, his or her blood pressure drops suddenly, and then he or she goes down: this is sin. Error is when the attraction or emotion brought about by a creature exerts an influence immediately stronger than something else that would propel freedom further ahead, that would make freedom move ahead. The attraction you feel isn't wrong. The error is preferring this attraction to the one that is weaker, yet leads more actively and surely towards destiny and introduces something to your heart, makes a proposal to your heart.

In the beginning, the vocation, that is, God's total plan for your lives, proposes things to you that normally, by their nature, are less attractive than dance clubs, girls, and companionship as your friends live it (including those of the Movement). But these things are the way you walk, by following, towards your destiny. The more you walk, the more attractive the things that represent your destiny become. The more you walk, the more magnificent the vocation will be.

It's the opposite of what happens with worldly things: the attraction is strongest at the outset, then it's over. Do you follow me or not? You have to repeat these things a hundred times. Either you discover them within yourself or, if they are taught, you should repeat them many times to discover them within yourself. You have to repeat them to understand them.

Freedom as a dynamic is provoked by creatures, therefore *omnis creature bona*.[9] Saint Paul said: everything is good, because everything calls us back to the Creator, each thing, all things. But some things can attract you more. Before the choice of something that you find less attractive but that brings you closer to your destiny, you are reasonably obligated to follow the second, not the first; if you don't do this, it's sin, error. This is so because freedom is still incomplete, so much so that it must be solicited through creatures, so much so that it can make mistakes. It is not yet complete, it's a freedom on a path. Freedom of choice is not freedom: it's an imperfect freedom. Freedom will be complete, full, when it's in front of the object that totally satisfies it. Then it will be totally free, total freedom.

3 THE CONDITIONS OF FREEDOM

As a final note: if you have a stronger attraction and God wants you here instead, what has to happen for you to renounce that attraction and come here?

a) The awareness of destiny
First: a clear awareness of destiny, love for destiny. If one loses sight of destiny, then he or she errs. Everyone, a hundred out of a hundred, lives like this; let's be attentive, because we too live like this. This is the horror, this is against man. It's inhuman. It's man living according to a criterion that is against man. That's what it seems like, and the whole world says: "It's right, it's comfortable, you deserve it, you want it, so do it!" No! Because life's destiny isn't that thing we want. It's the mystery of God, awareness of the Mystery, awareness of destiny.

b) Self-control
Second: we need a wrenching force, a force to wrench us from this attraction, so that you put your energy into moving towards your destiny. It's called mortification, capacity for mortification or penitence. Penitence is called *metanoia* in Greek and means "change of direction": instead of going here where you're more attracted, you have to make an effort to change direction, to change *nous*, to change the decision you need to make.

Thus: awareness of destiny – religious sense – and energy to dominate oneself – govern oneself – whose most critical aspect is called mortification or penitence. Tell me if these two things are possible for a person who's isolated. The companionship's most external and evident value – most clearly evident – is that it calls you back to the religious sense, to destiny.

Look, you don't hear even your mother say these things! Being reminded about destiny and self-governance, dominion over yourself: you govern yourself according to the destiny you are aware of. This always implies a tearing away, a wound. In Christian terms it's called penitence or mortification. Mortification means that it seems like a death, like a renunciation, but it isn't! Because if someone chooses this *T*, he then sees this *b* in another light, he doesn't lose it. He sees it in a permanent light, eternal, true and eternal, and loves with a love that is true and eternal. He no longer loses it; moreover, someone else will lose it, but he won't. Have you understood me?

I wanted to linger on the problem of freedom, because faith, as it pertains to the event of the Mystery that becomes man, becomes someone in the midst of things, in the midst of other people and things. Jesus was a man among others, a man amidst houses, amidst the country roads. He was a man in the crowd in Jerusalem, a man among other men. Think about John and Andrew: from the time they met that man, they went home to their wives and children, they went fishing – even the last chapter of Saint John speaks of them fishing at night – they went fishing, went to the synagogue with everyone else, went to Jerusalem, went out ... they did everything as they used to, but not as they used to. They had a figure within who stood between them and what they did: Him. He stood between their eyes and what their eyes beheld, between their heart and what they carried out, everything, in everything.

What does this ∞ have to do with? Everything! With hair: "Even the hairs of your head are counted,"[10] He said. It's the most beautiful thing He said, because nothing describes a contingent presence, a banal, concrete, material, ephemeral presence more than a hair that falls from the head. Likewise, the gaze with which He saw a flower in the field or a bird that falls – and all the more so of the child born to woman, a baby: "Woe to whoever scandalizes a child. It would be better for him to tie a millstone around his neck and throw himself into the deepest depths of the sea."[11] To harm a child both in the material sense and in the moral sense. In the material sense, everyone balks at harming children, but in the moral sense everyone harms children; they don't care, not even fathers and mothers. No one loves more than that man: He took a child in His arms, pressed Him to His chest and said that sentence. Faced with this scene, it's impossible to imagine a greater love for man. If a mother, the mother of that child, had her eyes sufficiently open, she should have felt, not "exonerated," but as if she were witnessing a love for her child that was greater than her own.

Jesus's call always entails entrusting yourselves to a community. Belonging to Christ always coincides with belonging to a community. These communities are like the arms of

Christ around that child, the eye of Jesus counting the hairs of your head, Jesus's eye that notices the falling sparrow or the small flower of the field, the powerful energy with which Jesus resuscitates the dead adolescent of the widow of Nain. But before and after, what was Jesus trying to do? Jesus was aiming at reviving the spirit of that woman: "Woman, don't cry."

The community is literally and physically Jesus, who does these things, Jesus present. So you learn what your destiny is in the community. The community gives you faith, sustains you in faith, governs and educates your faith, lets you understand what freedom is, and educates your freedom. It educates your freedom in the awareness of the developed religious sense and in the awareness of the sacrifices to make and, therefore, in the humble knowledge, and without the useless desperation, of your sin, of your sinning, of your ability to sin, of the ability to sin. Man has an enormous wound, shows the signs of an enormous wound, such that an arm that should have been able to lift sixty pounds can't lift six, as if it's weakened, as if it had a childhood paralysis. It's called original sin. So the community tells you not to be scandalized by temptation and not to be scandalized even at the mistakes you make, but to indomitably take up the path again. And together, we recognize what brings us to our destiny, we recognize what is great in life – what makes us move towards our destiny is great – and we recognize illusory attraction, the illusion of attraction. All this is an education the community gives you.

Now, what must we do with our freedom? The same thing we have to do with faith. What did the apostles have to do to learn and have faith in that man? They followed Him. If John and Andrew had only gone that one day, they would have had a great impression of Him. After ten years they would have told their kids, "We saw a man ...," but they wouldn't have had faith in that man. They followed Him. And how does one learn to be educated in freedom, so that freedom truly becomes the force in our life and therefore the dignity of our life (man's dignity lies in freedom, because freedom is a relationship with the infinite)? By following: by following the companionship in which the Lord, who calls us, has placed us. Following, nothing is more intelligent than following.

A Summary

Now we've seen what freedom is. We've seen that freedom is imperfect, it's on a path, imperfect; therefore you can choose. Why can you choose? Because it's imperfect. I used to make this observation in class: once your freedom gets here (∞), it's not blocked. It's completely wide open, it's all there. Here at (b), even though the attraction is great, freedom is blocked in a certain sense. There's some play inside, it doesn't really fit well, like a machine that's poorly assembled.[12] Since it has too much play inside, it can choose something else: choice is born from the fact that freedom is not yet itself.

So, we've seen what freedom is, we've seen the condition freedom is in. Freedom isn't choice, it's only a possibility to choose because it's imperfect. Insofar as freedom is the possibility to choose, it can aim for something it shouldn't, while instead it *must* only aim at what brings it to its destiny. This is moral law: that which brings it to destiny. Instead it chooses something that doesn't bring it to its destiny, it draws it away from destiny, and this is imperfection, error, sin. As if to say: they could've been so on the ball. What a shame ... they aren't.

Yet carrying out this correct choice demands a clear awareness of the relationship with Christ, of the relationship with destiny. It's the lived religious sense. Read the gospel, the first and twenty-first chapters of Saint John, when they're all together on that morning ... and Jesus had made breakfast for everybody – what care – and no one dared speak because they all knew it was the Lord. He's near Simon and He says to him, very softly, without the others realizing, He says quietly, "Simon, do you love me more than these?" This is the culmination of Christian morality: the beginning and the end of Christian morality. He didn't tell him, "Simon, you betrayed me. Simon, think how many mistakes you made. Simon, how many betrayals! Simon, just think that you can make the same mistake tomorrow and the day after ... Think about how fragile you are, what a coward you are in front of me." No! "Simon, do you love me more than these?" He went to the depths of everything, to the bottom of everything; so this *bottom of everything pulls everything along with it*. And Peter, who loved Him, ended up dying like Him. Go to page 408 of the text *Un avvenimento di vita, cioè una storia (An Event of Life, thus a History)* and find the phrase by Saint Thomas that says, more or less, that man finds his dignity in the choice of what he values most in life and from which he expects the greatest satisfaction.[13]

If you expect your satisfaction from something that can be dust tomorrow, you'll have dust. But who calls your attention to this? No one can, none of us has the strength to do it for himself: only together can we do it. This is the way that the Church, in the world, calls the world's attention to this. There could be a great, great man among us, nobler than Socrates and a greater orator than Demosthenes: he'd be speaking nonsense! The next day, he'd be in all the newspapers, everyone would think he's great, but no one would follow him. This mortification, or this appeal of *being*, which is the religious sense, is only recalled by the companionship. Only in the companionship are you recalled to this fascination with *being* or this awareness of our own fragility due to something that is a choice – to be able to choose is a good, but to be able to choose evil is an evil, therefore it's ambiguous. Freedom isn't in a bad position; it's in a position that is still ambiguous. It can choose good and it can choose evil. Only in the community is one helped to understand this, to be conscious of when one chooses evil, to recognize when one chooses evil, to have the strength of dominion over the self to wrench oneself from evil – for mortification, penitence or *metanoia*, change of mentality – to adhere to what brings us to destiny and to await destiny every day; to wait, every day, for it to come.

Invitation to Prayer

This is why you must, from now on, try to repeat the brief prayer that is emblematic of *Memores Domini*, *Veni Sancte Spiritus, Veni per Mariam* as frequently as possible. Come, O Spirit of the Immense, of the Mystery, because the Spirit of Mystery, the Spirit of Christ, is what allows us to understand things and gives us the energy to follow the right things. How does the Spirit of Christ help us? Through the viscera of a woman: Christ was born from the entrails of a seventeen-year-old girl, in other words, through the entrails of our common experience, of an experience in community. The Spirit communicates light and help to us through the entrails of a concrete experience.

ASSEMBLY
(revised January 1997)

We'll have you repeat words heard as discourse or words spoken as prayer that you don't understand. Not because we're fools and we make you do things that you don't understand. We know that you don't understand them. We didn't understand them either when we were young like you. Yet it's only by repeating them that you understand. What a two-year-old calls "mama" he'll refer to by the same word when he is fifty. That same word, not another word, will be profoundly different, understood more deeply, loved more deeply, judged more deeply ... but still one he has repeated his whole life long. The method we use to go to God is like this. This is how we come to terms with Christ.

This came to mind when I heard "We regard no one from the point of view of the flesh."[14] Do you remember reading this? You mean you don't remember it any longer, you've already forgotten it? "If one is in Christ, he is a new creature." If I were to say to you, "Explain this sentence to me," none of you – except some genius, still unknown – would be able to explain it to me. Would anyone be able to explain it to me?

If you don't know what it means, why repeat it? Because you're told to repeat it! And why are you told to repeat it? Because it's a form of asking. You know very well "who" you're asking. You're asking Christ. You don't understand the formula you use to ask. This will emerge in your experience as it matures over time.

It's not clear? This formula that you didn't understand is the formula of a question, of an asking for Christ. Is it right to ask for Christ? Is it right or not? Yes! But this question is formulated according to a type of awareness that requires maturity. That is why you will understand it as you become mature. Since you'll be using the question to ask Christ, you won't use it for naught: you'll use it to ask Christ. The formula isn't the important thing. What matters is asking for Christ. What is the greatest thing that man can do with all of his intelligence, and all of his freedom? Ask, or beg, which is the same thing. Because man is a poor little thing, and a poor little thing, whether a poor man or a little baby, can't do anything except ask. The little baby asks with everything that it says and does: it whimpers, cries, asks, holds out its hand, pulls on its mother's dress ... it asks.

Let's see, what was the theme of the last lesson? The foot? No!

Freedom

Come on, tell me. Who, at your age, has any instruction in freedom? And what about your friends? Up till now, have you had any? No one spoke to you about freedom! Everyone uses the word freedom, presuming a certain interpretation that is wrong. And it's not as if you've already learned what we've said. As if "said" equalled "learned." No, no! By repeating the clarifications, repeating the explanations, being attentive to the explanations that are repeated, eventually, a light that doesn't yet exist, or else, that barely exists, begins to enter into you.

What's the important thing? Even in this explanation, what's the important thing? To desire to understand; that is, to ask, to ask to understand, ask, always ask. There's no other richness than asking.

Asking is not demanding. Demanding asks even though it's already set its own conditions, already put forth its own measurements. You can't make demands of something that you don't know. You can only ask.

What does it mean that all creatures don't fulfill the breadth of my desire?

It means that they don't coincide with the total object of my desire. So first, my desire has too much room for movement and therefore, can choose; but above all, it tends to choose what attracts it more, the emotion that corresponds to it more, the momentary emotion more than the correspondence to destiny. It's natural!

But the most beautiful thing is the concept of tearing oneself away, and of mortification. Tearing yourself away from what excites you more for love of what corresponds to you more, that is more just – mortification to affirm the moral law (that is, the relationship with destiny instead of what attracts your instincts); this mortification doesn't eliminate anything: *omnis creatura bona* (everything is good). This sentence, says Charles Moeller in the introduction to *Sagesse grecque et paradoxe chrétien*,[15] is the greatest sentence in the history of human thought because the whole history of human thought divides what is good from what is bad, while Christianity says: evil isn't anything, there are no bad creatures; evil lies in the act of choice of what is in contradiction with your destiny. Evil is only in freedom's act of choice; for that reason, the factor of sin is man, it is man's freedom; but even this is dominated and overwhelmed by something else: by the fact that destiny takes you back and calls you back, and gives you the energy to start again and be called back. He came to give you personally this energy to start again and be called back: it's the community in which you live within the Church, to which you belong; He lets you belong to a community in which He helps you thus. The community is what you belong to: it's more than father, mother, family.

Is unfulfilled freedom also towards Christ?
Unfulfilled freedom is unfulfilled freedom. Freedom is imperfect before anything: before itself, in the face of destiny, before Christ, before one's mother, before one's father, before one's friend ... it's imperfect before everything; its imperfection is in play with anyone and therefore its imperfection is in play with Christ.

It's because of this that Christ can seem to be without all the attractiveness that He should have: because freedom turns the eyes towards something else and so He doesn't appear for what He is. To understand how He is, you need to look hard at Him: Andrew and John, when they were there, while He was speaking, you think they were looking at the furniture? Were they looking at the paintings that were hanging there? They were there to watch Him: they watched Him speak. And because their freedom was imperfect, their adherence to what He said was shaky, was fragile, but it was there, it was desired.

Sure, we're even imperfect with Christ. Moreover, we're much more imperfect with Christ than with the others. Why? Because of original sin: we have that wound in us, that infantile paralysis that increases in proportion to the greatness of the object we are in relationship with. The more it's great and worthy, the more this wound is in play. Original sin is not a lack of something, as if God had made a flawed creature; rather, original sin is an act of man, who God made so linked to all other men that the flawed beginning reverberated through everything.

At school, I used to make this comparison. Imagine the seam of this table: if it's on the floor, you can easily walk on it, even almost without looking. But if you take this seam and raise it up to a hundred metres, your head will spin and you won't be able to do it anymore – unless you're a superhuman acrobat with lots of training. But if you raise the seam to a thousand metres, even the acrobat will fall.[16] Original sin is an existential condition for which the individual man is not guilty, but for which he bears the consequences: the one who committed it is the guilty one. And how he committed it, and what it consisted of, this is a mystery, the mystery of the origins. "Mystery" is an annoyance, but if you don't admit to this mystery, you can't understand anything about the disaster of man. Man is a disaster: the doctrine of original sin explains this disaster in the most adequate way conceivable.

When work is burdensome, tiring, how can freedom be put into play within this situation?

When I have a burdensome duty to perform, what does my freedom do to enter into something so burdensome? Look, tell me the most difficult thing that exists. Death. You know that Jesus was murdered, and unjustly so. What did He do there to put His freedom into effect?

Accept! Accept the project of Another, which is the will of God: "Father, if it is possible that I not die, [He said, showing Himself to be a man like me], but may it be that not my, but your will be done [showing that He had a freedom immensely more powerful than mine],"[17] making me also able to say "May Your will be done" when faced with a burdensome task. Is this clear? Is this attitude intelligent or submissive? Is it an intelligent attitude to say: "I accept something that is hard" as the cross was for Christ? Why is it right or – better still – reasonable to do the will of God in something hard, that in the end, makes you die?

Because it's correspondent.

Correspondent to what?

To your needs for happiness.

Dying is correspondent to your needs for happiness?

To the mission that was entrusted to you.

So the hard work to do is a mission that was entrusted to you. By whom? By God. Through the master, by God; through Pontius Pilate, master of the Hebrew people back then, for a few years, it's from God that that task was entrusted to Christ. Therefore, it's something intelligent, that is, reasonable, that corresponds precisely to the heart because it corresponds to the will of God: to correspond to the will of God means to correspond to one's own destiny, to walk towards one's own destiny. What makes you walk towards your destiny is reasonable. And your destiny is the mystery of God.

Now, pardon me – I absolutely have to ask you this: what is freedom? The capacity for relationship with destiny. Destiny, what is destiny? Let's ask an easier question: where does destiny exist? Destiny exists at the end of life. Milan-Como highway: where does Como begin? Where the highway for Como ends! Milan-Pavia road: the road ends where Pavia begins. The end is the first thing one has in mind: when they begin to build a road, the thing that they have in mind is the end, destiny (that is Pavia). Then, they build the road, they work, work, work ... they reach Pavia: the work is finished! Destiny is at the end of the road, that is, it's on the other side of the last stretch of road, it's on the other side of death. Everything that brings us to the end, towards destiny, is reasonable; what corresponds to the heart is not the instincts you feel, but rather, what brings your heart towards its destiny; and what brings your heart towards its destiny can be a life of suffering and sorrow.

I'm sure they didn't have you read *Life and Fate*.[18] Not one of you has read it. Get it, and in three years, you'll finish it! In it, the life of the Russian people under Stalin is described; it's a historic, dramatic, and terrific book: it's a book worthy of Dostoevsky. Their lives are all massacred and crushed, yet it was either right for them to commit suicide or right for them to live. It was right for them to live because in living, they were accepting, without knowing, the path that led to their destiny. To live is reasonable; otherwise, when things go badly, it would only be reasonable to shoot yourself in the temple: no way!

You said: it's necessary for the infinite to reach man in order to activate his freedom; so this destiny is already here. I want to know if the experience of perfect freedom as an adhesion to totality is possible now, even within the choice.

Adhesion to destiny is the meaning of every step that you take along the path. Path: you can take your steps towards destiny, maybe a little more slowly, more timidly, a little more weakly; however, you're taking steps towards destiny. Each step towards your destiny is a step towards the whole destiny (there isn't a half destiny or three-quarters destiny), but the immediate object of your will and action isn't the presence of destiny in its total final expression, therefore you can't be satisfied – you can only become more satisfied than if you had done the opposite: "Whoever follows me will have life eternal [and this is destiny] and a hundredfold here below."[19]

The way we will love in heaven is a way that can only be foreseen and understood by those who truly, intensely, and faithfully loved, with their whole selves, others in this world. Those who have loved their own neighbours with their whole selves, with all their faithfulness, with all their force of will, with all their capacity for sacrifice, in other words, with all their affectivity, can better foresee, better imagine how heaven will be – but it's not yet heaven.

Therefore, those who follow Him will have a hundredfold here below. I've said this from the first year I taught religion in high school: a hundredfold here below means that you will love your girlfriend a hundred times more, you will love your boyfriend a hundred times more, you will love your father and mother a hundred times more, you will love your classmates a hundred times more; you've been together five years, and there's complete estrangement, there's no friendship between you, there's only conniving: conniving to get into mischief, or conniving to go to the mountains together on Saturday and Sunday, but there isn't friendship, because friendship is to pour out your life into the life of another. Therefore: those who follow Him, who follow destiny, who reach towards destiny, will have it; they will reach their destiny and will also have the hundredfold here below.

In Guido Clericetti's third book (I hope that you have his first two books with jokes that are oftentimes observations at a really high level of humour, and great humour is always sadness. For example, this one: "Anniversary: I can read between your lines."[20] It makes you want to cry. I can read between your lines. But anyway, a third one came out, and they're all phrases like this, almost all of them) the back cover has a drawing of a starry sky and underneath is written: "Connect the dots between these stars and you'll have the finished drawing." Destiny is connecting the dots between all things, and this will happen only at the end, because it's only possible from another point of view: from the point of view of the one who makes the stars. "He who follows me will have eternal life and a hundredfold here below," he'll know how to enjoy those stars a hundred times more.

Which happened to me one time when I was chaplain of the Milanese colony they have in Celle Ligure: I was there in the winter as chaplain because I had been sick, and I had some beautiful experiences. For example, I used to go every evening from Celle Ligure to Varazze and back again. There, there's a loop along the coast, a stretch of shore with a low retaining wall, then there's the beach and the sea. On a spring evening, the wall was packed with young couples, and I passed by many times, and said: "Who knows, who knows these poor kids, these poor kids that live here without knowing why they live, of what they live, and they therefore live by instinct (but all men are like this)." One evening the moon wasn't out, but there was an absolutely clear sky, full of stars. Just as I turned the corner of the street, I saw what none of you has ever seen, at the beach. In the morning I woke the children up, saying: "Let's go to see the bridge on the sea! The bridge on the sea!"[21]

Then everybody got up in a hurry (otherwise it would have taken a half hour to get them up). Well, I saw, I stayed there dumbstruck to see it: the bridge of light cast on the sea by the Milky Way. Then I thought: "It's really true that there's a hundredfold here below. Who knows how to look at the sea to this degree? Who knows how to observe things to this degree? None of these people." Understand? The Milky Way that forms a bridge on the sea, just barely highlighted, but decidedly highlighted, without the strength of the moon, which is like that of the sun; not just any reflection, but really a bridge of light. The bridge of light on the sea with the Milky Way – none of you has ever seen it, has ever observed it, has ever discovered it, nor will you ever discover it if you don't pay attention to things such as love for destiny, which is Christ, which makes us capable of doing it.

During these days, I realized that I've had some experience in respect to people, having had the possibility to look more at their destiny. But being precisely aware that my freedom, like everyone's, is limited, I'd like to ask whether this experience of freedom is strictly tied even to the experience of grace!

The experience of freedom, in as much as you look at a creature in relationship to its destiny – and therefore, to your destiny, because destiny is one sole thing for everybody – is an act on your part. You understand that it's yours, so much so that maybe you would be tempted to look at him or her in another way but you don't do it because you judge the situation and say: "OK, in another way ... and then what?"

But if you hadn't found a certain companionship, if you hadn't heard certain discourses, if your mother hadn't made you learn the Our Father, if whoever made you hadn't given you a certain sensibility of spirit, you'd also be leaden, squat, rough, clumsy, like most of your friends, and you would have spoken about that creature with the same rudeness, with the same repugnance that many people do when they talk (many guys when they talk about women, etc.). Meaning, then, that it's not a pure choice of your freedom, thoroughly plain and simple: it's your freedom that adheres to a complex of clues and positive stimuli that it already has inside. This is freedom: to adhere to what impels you towards what is just and what is good.

The thing that permits this is called grace; it's grace to have a certain character of a certain sensibility, with a certain instinctive repugnance to coarseness, it's a grace to have learned the Our Father, it's a grace to have found certain friends, it's a grace for you to have heard someone say

"Come," an incomparable grace, so much so that now you can foresee something, but how much more time you need to understand it! Passing time, that's a grace!

But, even having had this grace, your freedom could have been so capricious, so rebellious, so nihilistic, so restless, so instinctive, so fond of the instinct that is always inside you as to say no to everything that the sensibility of the Our Father and the companionship suggests to you.

That you may have said yes, therefore, is the fruit of a previous grace (that from before) and is the fruit of an immanent grace at the moment of choosing, at the moment of acting, at the moment in which you accept thinking about destiny. It's always grace that prepares you and sustains you in the moment. For that reason, your freedom lies much more in asking Christ that grace may enlighten and sustain you in the opportune moment, rather than in saying: "Christ, let me do it: I'll worry about it; when the moment comes, I'll do it." This presumption would take a heavy toll.

What characterizes a spirit that loves the destiny of things, that is, a free spirit that lives the dimension of freedom, is a characteristic that is very human, that is found in the simple of heart. You find it a lot in the poor, and when you find it in a rich person or an intelligent and cultured man, it's truly a miracle. It is gratitude: gratitude, a hint of gratitude, like a piece of gratitude, a sliver of gratitude, a touch of gratitude precisely in the act; but it's in everything that one does, which is the most beautiful thing that can be noticed in the face and in the attitude of the person. What a little friar sang in a modest little play in the seminary has remained with me: "God sees goodness more than He sees the face." Man is also like this. Man sees goodness more than he sees the face, because it's more real, it's more consequential and tangible; goodness is more imposing than the solid or flimsy structure of the facade.

Last time, in the lesson on freedom, you told us: "Tell me if these things are possible for an isolated person." Therefore, I want to ask you what weight, what attention we have to give to this new companionship of ours during the week – in what way is it right away a part of the very nature of the things we are speaking about.

OK, first of all – the first aspect of the question – can this freedom be recognized and lived alone? Theoretically, yes; existentially, it's impossible – save a miraculous exception – because alone, man is the prey of the environment he lives in, and only by an awesome intervention of God can an individual be saved from the environment, from the environment's physical model and way of thinking, from the normal habits of the environment in which he lives. First of all, then, alone, it is immensely – let's say it like this – more difficult that freedom be perceived and grasped in such a way that it can be lived.

If alone it's so difficult, together it becomes easier. Together – what does that mean? When you happen to walk the same road with others; and when this companionship with others is guided and formed, guided and sustained by a reminder of what is right, what is true, by a calling back to what freedom truly is, by a reminder of the destiny we're made for, in other words by a religious reminder, by a Christian reminder. When you are in a companionship where the Christian reminder is made and where people adhere to that very companionship because inside it that reminder exists; moreover, where people adhere because they feel the same vocation. So, to understand what freedom is and, above all, to live it, becomes easier.

Anna lives in a certain place, teaches in a school, and works on a particular course at the university. If she picks up the telephone and you're home because on Wednesday you have school until twelve, or else on Saturday because you're off from work, she asks: "How's it going?" You're surprised that a person that you've never seen until now is calling you; you don't even remember any longer that she was the group leader, and you're very pleased that she has called you. She tells you: "Take heart! Listen, even I had to muster up courage, not only yesterday, but even now. Therefore, for you to have courage, ask the Blessed Mother, ask the Spirit for the grace to understand. What we said, for example, last time, on freedom, ask the Spirit to understand it because it's extremely important." Maybe you were in a difficult situation with your father, with your mother, with a guy whose nose you liked, and you thank her. "Bye." "Bye." You put the phone down and say: "No, I have to be firmer" and you become firmer with the guy whose nose attracted you. You understand?

The companionship – for example, when you go to the mountains, the companionship is a reciprocal calling back (if you're in company, you remind people, "Be careful here, be careful there," you speak with one person, you speak with another); the companionship is a reciprocal calling back to destiny, to the aim, or to the vitality, or to the gladness, or to the purity of things – it helps you to act with freedom, it lets you better understand what freedom is.

"You know, Anna, I didn't understand this thing here about the wide line and the narrow line: the narrow line is the higher one, the wide line is the lower one to the right, and well, I'm more attracted by the wide line on the bottom. What do I do to choose the line which is up high and to the left, which is narrower?" Then, she explains to you why the drawing isn't perfect – as was also said by the one who did it, that you needed two dimensions, even he isn't a fool – and, as she is explaining it to you, the idea of freedom grabs you more. It's in this way that you learn. After years of this companionship, you are different, different from the others: at work, you are different from the others; at school, you are different from the others; at college you are different from the others; in the family, you become different from the others. You understand, reason, feel, work, face things in a way different from others. You are a person. Saint Paul would say you are a new person, because in Christ Jesus it doesn't mean anything to be Greek, or to be Jewish (the big ideal division of that time), but what matters is the new creature, a new way to think and to feel.[22] After a few years – but what am I saying, years; month to month you become different, even if you don't understand how.

I began GS in freshman year of high school at Berchet and, during the whole year, not even the dogs came around my students; therefore I held my meetings with just a few kids from the school – there were seven or eight – that I had encountered in the street and that were faithful to me. At the end of the year, I went to the principal and said: "Listen, Mr Principal, they do exercises in physics in the physics classroom, but for religion, there isn't a classroom to do religious "exercises," so at the end of the year, I'll do religious "exercises" – I'll take them away for three days with me." I didn't tell him that it was spiritual exercises, I said that it was "religious experimentation." And I brought them to a beautiful place, a Moorish palace on Lake Orta, near Orta. There were about sixty of them.

At a certain point, I was saying that life grows slowly, that you don't see life growing. For example, my mother, when we went on vacation, stood me in front of a particular tree as soon as we arrived, and marked it with a knife to see the point I reached. Then, after three months, she brought me in front of the tree, and you saw that in three months, I had grown this much. And every year it was like this: in other words, the tree was full of these markings. Life grows, but you don't see it growing. Everybody was there with faces a little strange, they didn't understand. "But how can it be, you don't understand this thing here? Outside – all of you!" Then, I brought them outside, and there was a really beautiful bed of Dutch tulips not yet completely in bloom. "Look at these flowers: are they alive or dead?" "Alive." "If they're alive, they are moving, life is moving. Stare at them: when you see them move, tell me." They stayed there ... and I left! They were there, baffled, and I came back after two minutes, a minute and a half, and I said: "I could leave you here all day today and tomorrow, you'd become statues, but you wouldn't ever be able to see life grow; nevertheless it grows." One step in life's development is infinitesimal. The development of life is like a mask that hides the mystery, the mystery of life as such.

In this way, you'll learn – with the passing of months, years – these things. If you follow. Everyone that came and at a certain point said: "Yes, you may also be right, but I'm sick and tired, I'm leaving," didn't learn after that. Those who remained, learned. This is an incredible thing: those who remain, learn, become themselves; those who don't remain, lose themselves.

Creatures draw out freedom. I often feel pulled by so many things, so many things I'd like to do, occasions, situations I'd put myself into, and I'd like reality to move forward with a good project. How, instead, can you purify the gaze with which you ask, in things, to be an instrument? Where does vocation enter in, then, with this desire to get involved with everything?

If a creature, as we said last time, is a reverberation of the infinite perfection of being or of the Mystery, even a blade of grass, even the pine tree, the pine needle. When I was a little kid in elementary school, in the mountains during the summer, I tormented my mother with this question: "But does the Lord know the number of all these leaves that are in all the trees in the world?" My mother, a little stuck, said, "Umm, yes!" And it was really an insurmountable objection for me that someone could know the number of all the pine needles and all the pine trees in the world. Nevertheless, the principle remains as it is: every created thing is a reverberation of the perfection, of the ocean of perfection, of the boundless perfection of the mystery of Being. And it's not just a reverberation like light, like a projector; it's not like a projector where you put something in front of it and it projects the shape, no; it's the nature of the entire pine needle, that's the reflection of the Mystery; the pine tree needle doesn't make itself in any moment.

If, then, every creature is a reflection of the richness of God, you, the more sensitivity you have, the more you're pulled in every direction: by what's big, by what's small, by what presses on you from the front, by what crushes you, by what pushes you from behind, from everywhere.

The first problem: how do we know what to choose in that moment, in a determined moment? This, as you said, is the problem of vocation: you're obliged to choose what God indicates as useful – if not necessary – to the vocational task He's entrusted to you. For example, if you have a life dedicated to the Lord and you're a science professor at school, your vocation is that of dedicating yourself to the Lord totally, even being a science teacher at school. If you're a science teacher, you'll have to explain pine needles as well as you can. Therefore it's your vocation that establishes the fact that you must interest yourself in the pine needle, make the students study, instead of having the luck and the grace to interest yourself, like Professor Vera, in Mozart or Beethoven. There's no other way to respond: through the circumstances, if your attitude is open and attentive to God, He makes you see what's useful or better for your vocation, including your work, because work is a complete part of vocation.

Can we say that freedom is like the decision or position of desiring that the wonder generated by the encounter remain?
I would say that freedom is the active and affective willingness to see that exceptionality and that greatness of relationship that constituted your first encounter re-proposed in all your relationships.

This observation is very important: the encounter because of which one entered the movement or Gruppo Adulto was perhaps hardly hinted at, almost unconscious; but no one can say someone grabbed you by the throat and dragged you. No! If you're here, it's because something struck you: weakly, but it struck you. And it struck you through a presentiment at least, a presentiment of exceptionality or, as the Bible says, a promise of happiness. A promise that, in the mentality of the Hebrews of that time, coincided with the multiplication of fertility.

Freedom is favouring the intellectual, affective, and creative willingness to perceive and correspond to the Presence that dictated your beginning and that – whatever you see in the world and whatever condition you're in, whatever day you wake up, even your worst exam day – is taken into account. What makes the burden of studying reasonable is the same reason that you fell in love with Christ.

Regarding the graph you drew for us last time, we were asking ourselves where Jesus Christ is in it, exactly inasmuch that – as you just said – it's God who concretely takes part in history, in flesh and bone. The trajectory of freedom that moves towards its destiny and encounters creatures is described there.

In whatever point of the graph. Christ is nothing other than the incarnation – the becoming flesh, born of a woman – of the utmost line, meaning, of the utmost term that defines freedom. Freedom is the capacity for relationship with the infinite. We've signified the infinite with the highest line: that line is the Word, it's the Mystery that became flesh. Flesh means a small baby, therefore even a trace of a centimetre; or, become flesh, He threw His reflection on the manner in which you see the starry sky and it seems that it's a larger expanse of sky.

So then, the infinite becomes flesh means that the infinite enters into the only great experience of history, which is the reality of Being, the reality of the Mystery, lived by men, on a human scale. Therefore, in all things, you find the concrete reverberation of Christ, because what are you made of? What is a pine tree made of? What's a little bird made of? "Everything subsists in Him." Thus, if you watch a small bird, just as Christ watched it, you are awed, you marvel at the thing, just as you marvelled when you read that passage that time or, hearing I don't know whom, you understood that Christ was true: it's a great thing in the same way.

If you hear a bird, for example a nightingale, as did the missionary with whom I took my first trip to Macapá near the edge of the Amazon River, where there were no streets, nothing (there were only snakes); he heard a nightingale – and while we were travelling in a jeep, he told me his story. He lived two hours away by jeep from the centre of the mission, a little city of thirty thousand people, Macapá. And I asked him: "But aren't you afraid being there?" "No, you get used to it, and then, every fifteen days I return to the mission [for a day of rest with his confreres]." He had, back then, an extremely rare Guzzi 750 motorcycle; few of them were around, he adored it so much that he told me that, when it started to rain (because there it rains suddenly, then stops), he covered the motorbike, not himself, with his cloak. One night when he was there stretched out, tired, with the motorbike parked with the cloak over it, and was listening to a nightingale – because "there are nightingales here, too and they have the same song as they do where we live, only the last part is missing," he told me; he had noticed that there, the nightingale's song lacked a final piece of the melody, it was like a suspension of the melody. While he was listening to the nightingale he heard the roar of a leopard approaching. So he hurried up: got on the motorbike and escaped. And while he was leaving, the leopard, with one pounce, was right there where he had been. But that kind of missionary, who looked at everything like that, not only the nightingale, but everything, was an open freedom, available to recognize the Mystery of Christ in all things, and the reality of creation became for him a marvel, in everything, even in a blade of grass, just as for Jesus, even the teeth of the decayed dog.[23]

Thus, that God became man doesn't mean at all that he became that man and that was it. That man is a generative factor in all the history of humanity, affecting the whole development of history, so much so that Saint Paul compares Him with everything: "Everything consists in Him."[24]

But I understand perfectly the alteration, literally the alteration, that all these examples should provoke in you, because it's another mentality; what we're talking about is another mentality, that is, another culture, it's another vision, perception, affection, use of the world: it's another world! A world where God is man, is present and eats at the same table with me – Eucharist – it's another world. It's another world; only this world is true and the other is false, and this is so true that those others do not keep their promises: "they have ears but do not hear, they have eyes but do not see, they have mouths but do not speak"; they don't keep any of the promises they make.[25]

Can you explain again what it means that freedom is imperfect? What is freedom?

The capacity to reach destiny, to enter into relationship with the Mystery.
Therefore freedom is fulfilled when it reaches the goal. There is freedom, there is all of freedom; freedom is fulfilled, freedom is complete when it reaches the goal: before, it's imperfect. It's imperfect, but all of its dynamic is intent on reaching destiny – on fulfilling itself. A child is not a man, but his whole dynamic is intent on becoming a man.

Everything consists in reaching the goal: you said that, for the Milan–Pavia highway, the goal is when the highway finishes at Pavia; then what does the value of the highway consist of?
The value of the highway is in the correct use of the motor, of cars ... if you get in a car patched with cotton, you probably won't go three feet. The road is useful for understanding whether your intention and your recognition of desiring the goal are true, and of your love for the goal, and your capacity to use freedom for this goal. It's called test. Peguy, in *The Mysteries*, insists upon life as a trial: the road is for testing.[26]

But deep down, my friend, is it a sign of greater affection on the part of God if He takes man and makes him His companion on the road to overcome the trial, or if He makes him already perfect? A plant that's already packaged is an artificial plant. A plant, to not be artificial, has to come out of the ground, slowly, according to all its laws. So, to not be superficial or in the clouds, man's happiness should also come from his freedom: from his freedom and from the hand of God.

Imagine a father who comes home from work – still works in the fields, poor thing; not poor thing, he's lucky! – comes home from work and his wife left the smallest kid, who is four years old, in his care. And the smallest kid wants to help dad carry the hay. The father has a basket full of hay on his back, the little kid has his handful of hay and, all proud, follows dad, but it takes the father three hours longer. So it is with God, but it's Saint Peter's observation: God has patience to test the freedom of each one of you.[27]

You say that freedom is given by the breadth of desire and by one's capacity to satisfy it, and one of man's desires is that for work. Because of this, one without work is more easily depressed, is less free. Since so many of our friends are having a hard time trying to find work, how should we look at this time?
First: work is an essential expression of man's life and it's the essential way he imitates God – *Pater meus usque modo operatur* (my Father is the eternal worker)[28] – without now counting the punishment of original sin.[29] Now, people esteem their work that much more the more they are available to give all their energy to what God asks of them.

The ultimate rule isn't that one has to work at this or that thing, but that one obey God. Christ's great work was obedience to the Father. When Father Kolbe was taken and put in that den where he died with all the other poor people he had tried to uphold right to the end, he didn't work as before, he was called to another work, a much greater one: he did the will of the Father. We are called not to work, but to do the will of the Father. The will of the Father implies, as a normal factor in the development of life, work.

Second: what work — these people who don't have work should ask this — what work? What the Father has them find. Now, first, they should go around and concern themselves with this problem, not make others worry about it while they sit there with their hands folded. Second, if the ideal job for them is not available, they must even be a dishwasher: washing dishes is work; not doing anything isn't work.

Thus, work isn't the value of life, the value of life is obedience; in obedience, the commitment to work is also implied.

So to do the will of the Father means to look for the conditions in which the Father permits us to find work: not letting others do the searching, but searching ourselves with everyone's help. Until you find work that you like — that expresses you — it's love and obedience to the Father to accept even work that expresses you less and that you like less.

For example, imagine a priest like poor Monsignor Manfredini, archbishop of Bologna, my classmate. The superiors in the seminary, worried because he was a little bit too free when he said Mass, sent him to a hole just outside Milan, and it was very difficult for him, he was discouraged. One stroke of luck concerning my relationship with him was that I was the only one who went to see him some days after, and we thus reestablished that friendship that had defined our whole history in the seminary. But a man of his type would have guided a big church beautifully, and they gave him a little second-rate parish of a few hundred people, so that when his mother saw me she cried. And he accepted this, he accepted it, setting a great example. If he hadn't accepted it, maybe he wouldn't have become archbishop of Bologna.

Problem number one is obedience, but we still haven't talked about that.

Before, you said: what makes the burden of study reasonable is the same reason for which you fell in love with Christ.
There's a reason why I fell in love with Christ. Christ tells me "Study." And I study, I obey him: what kind of love is it if I don't obey Him?

The reason I'm in love with Christ is because of the exceptionality I recognized?
Absolutely! And this exceptional man tells you: "Cast your nets on the other side," "Don't waste time," or, according to the more down-to-earth translation of Saint Paul: "He who doesn't work, doesn't eat."[30] Therefore tell your friends who don't have work to hurry up and find it. This stresses that whether it's this work or that work is beside the point: just work.

Now, how did I confront the question? Saying that work is fundamental for a Christian conception of a life dedicated to God. Second: that therefore everyone should look for a job. Third: that a job has value even if it isn't according to your likes. One looks according to one's likes, doesn't find a job according to one's likes, then looks according to other criteria: it's enough just to have a job; no, it's enough to look seriously for a job (from this you can't deduce that you'll succeed in finding one; if it were only this way, all of today's unemployment problems wouldn't exist!).

I'm saying that a situation in which a man in a Gruppo Adulto house is without work can't be tolerable: period, closed case! No, he finds anything, as long as he works: he'll go serve the parish of the nearby church, be a sacristan, clean floors without even earning five cents, but he must have a job. My attitude, evidently, does not involve accusing anyone, but rather affirms the necessity of work! Without work, an individual atrophies and lies to his or her own life. For example, if a man looks for work for months and isn't able to find anything, he should, in the meantime, take whatever comes his way. Instead of working three months in a row, he might work three weeks in a row, or a week every three months. But it's the house that, first of all, should get involved in helping people who don't have work to find it; it can't simply be the individual who doesn't have work who has to pull up his sleeves and get to work. It's the whole companionship that has to be interested in him having work. And if the house isn't enough, all of Gruppo Adulto should get involved in finding work for this individual. In the meantime, this individual does what he can. I'm not accusing those poor things who, given the social conditions, have to suffer to the point of having the humiliation of not succeeding at finding work. I'm not scolding them. I'm underlining the urgency that should find them first in line to get themselves, the house, and all of their friends moving so that the development of their life may consider and contain this inevitable obligation to be what God wants.

The need for work. Not at all the prevalent need of what you like, even if you should first of all look for something you like. Why first of all must you look for something you like? Because if you like it, it's – a priori – a more pressing invitation, a more immediate invitation that God gives you. And if you like it, probably, you'll turn out more, you would turn out more, but these optimal conditions aren't necessary.

The dean of my faculty, when I said Mass, gave me a book called *Prêtre et hostie* (*Priest and Host*),[31] in which the sickness of a deacon was described, a sickness that lasted twenty-five years, in which his work consisted of the consciousness with which day by day he tried to live his sickness, offering it to God in remission for the world. This is a job. Because work is the application to reality – a reality which is so much more energized towards its destiny – of the consciousness and affectivity and the constructive activity of a man who lives the faith. *Et de hoc satis* (and that's enough about that).

I would like to understand this sentence better: freedom is carried out in possession.
How was freedom defined? Capacity for adhering to Being, capacity for adhesion to the totality of Being, capacity for adhesion to the end, to destiny. Now, if freedom is this capacity for adhesion, there is more freedom the more one possesses being, possesses reality. For this reason, virginity is a greater possession due to the totality of devotion.

To possess means to enter into relation at the level of being with another thing. Freedom is adhering to reality. If you go out and say: "This is earth with gravel," it's an act of reason, you perceive evidence. Reason is adhering to reality; adhering to reality means affirming it: it's the beginning of possessing it.

It's a different way from adhering physically: this is an exterior aspect; there's no need to stretch yourself out on the ground and "adhere" to the dirt and the stones: "But I adhere to the earth!" Why would it be irrational if you did that? It would be irrational because it's inhuman, it's not the human way of adhering.

There's possession that isn't physical, that isn't of purely physical contact. That's only one aspect of possession. You have to possess a piece of bread physically to eat it, but this is the more animalistic kind of possession that exists in man (you see certain ways of relating between boys and girls, of relations between one person and another).

It's another way of relating, but it's possession: that the affirmation of reality is a possession is indicated by the fact that you affirm and explain what that reality is, you understand it, you can use it according to its capacity for performance and, if it's a person, you love it (for this reason love is free, greater, deeper than time and space, that is, than the physical relation you can have). The physical relation isn't ownership: you can't penetrate a person to the roots of his or her soul, but if you look at him or her or think of the person when he or she is away, you possess him or her down to the roots of the soul.

Man has a way of possessing that, on one hand, touches that of the animal and, on the other, touches − even if it's a state just hinted at − the possession of God. God possesses the stones and the earth and every leaf and every sparrow that falls and every flower of the field. But not because He's on top of the flower of the field. He's at the root of the flower of the field, He's within it. Man's possession is similar to that of God.

If freedom is the capacity for adhesion, the more one adheres, the more it's freedom; and the more it's freedom, the more one possesses, because to adhere means to possess.

There's only one alternative to Christ, nothing. I would like you to explain this sentence to me better.
Why did Christ come? The *School of Community* says that Christ came to educate humanity to its religious sense, that is, to educate humanity to understand, to affirm, to acknowledge that there's an ultimate purpose to all the movement of things.[32] This ultimate purpose is God. Thus, Christ came to educate man in the religious sense; Christ came to educate man to do everything as a function of his destiny.

If you take the Antichrist, the non Christ, instead of Christ, as a working hypothesis, you take as a working hypothesis something that, as such, doesn't adhere to anything. If freedom according to Christ is the adhesion to Being, to the Mystery of things – and therefore, life is completely positive – even evil is made to be something positive. Everything is good. "Everything was good, even my evil," said Ada Negri, discovering the idea that converted her.[33] If freedom is adhesion to being, that is, the apprehension of being, grasping being, possession of being, if you don't have this working hypothesis (freedom is adhesion to being), what other hypothesis can you have? That freedom isn't adhesion to being. So, either it's a fake invention of being part of reality, a false invention of existing, a nervous and negative affirmation of what doesn't exist, or at that point – as in the true alternative – the working hypothesis of life is that everything in life is bad: "For me this life is bad," said Leopardi.[34]

Therefore, either the hypothesis of freedom is something that reacts to the existent, to life, or this hypothesis is positive and brings one to reality as something constructed, so even pain and death become instruments of construction; or it's negative and then even the good becomes bad; even the good becomes bad because, in the very end, it becomes ashes, even the good becomes ashes; it's useless to get involved: "Go up then, Thou, Thou mighty man of mettle."[35]

Speaking of imperfect freedom, you said that we can choose the right thing with the consciousness of destiny. If I think about the choices I've made to arrive here, at this point in my life, the consciousness of destiny was probably very far off.
A clear consciousness of why you took certain steps could have been far away, but you took these steps for an ultimate, positive hypothesis of life, otherwise you wouldn't have taken them, right? What was the question?

It seems that I had chosen without this consciousness of destiny.
I have already responded to this. Explicit consciousness of destiny – it could have been confused, but you took these steps because you chose what emerged to you – albeit in a confused way – as better, as more useful, as truer. Thus you had the consciousness of destiny, only it wasn't clear yet, it wasn't yet self-aware.

Clear consciousness of destiny isn't necessary to walk towards the truth of your destiny. You can choose things that bring you towards your destiny even simply for the terror that "without this, what's left?" Saint Peter: "Lord, if we go away from you, where shall we go? Only you have the words that explain life."[36] Because, if you eliminate the positive hypothesis, you're left with the negative hypothesis: where would we end up? This second position is never rational, because it doesn't explain, it's never a comprehensive reason for everything. To affirm the negative aspect, a negative solution, is never rationality, never, because reason is consciousness of reality according to all the factors that carry it towards its destiny. If a child – I've already mentioned this comparison – growing up, found itself in front of the hypothesis: "But was my mother really killed during the war or is she still here?" (because there are signs that allow for some doubt), to eventually be able to find her, the child has to use a positive hypothesis. With negative hypotheses nothing is brought to a conclusion, you wouldn't discover anything, science wouldn't advance, technology wouldn't advance.

You said "Either Christ or nothing." Existentially, can you say that even the whole dynamic of freedom is absolutely unimaginable without Christ?

Without Christ it would be something one would feel was right, more natural, but you wouldn't have the elements for a certain clarity, you wouldn't have, above all, the fundamental element, that is, the courage to affirm it.

Is this a problem of method?

That, to resolve a problem, you need to use a positive hypothesis, not a negative one, is the most serious question of method that one can cite.

I understood this in an experience I had in school that I've already talked about elsewhere. In mathematics, I always got Ds and Fs, because I never did well in it. I thought I was faithful in my studying, but in reality, I wasn't really studying, because I was studying in a detached way, without any interest, without *inter-esse,* without being inside the question. This went on until freshman year of high school, when a disciple of Enrico Fermi, his favourite disciple, arrived. His name was don Borghi. In the first homework assignment he gave us six problems: a point off for every problem done wrong, four points off for getting them all wrong – he had an irresolvable problem. In working it out, we had to demonstrate that it was irresolvable. All of us, instinctively, began with a positive hypothesis; therefore, all of us solved it! Next class, he said: "I'm telling you that the first problem is the irresolvable one. You have to demonstrate it so." Everyone got an F, because no one was sure that they had done the problem correctly. When it was over, it seemed to have gone well, then everyone went back to see whether we had made any mistakes. We went over it three, four, five times until an hour had gone by.

You get it? Starting from a negative hypothesis impedes you from solving something; so much so that when you start with a negative idea that life is meaningless, life is lacking, life is something less, no one will have children anymore.[37]

What difference is there between this negative hypothesis that blocks us and the melancholy temperament that is defined as positive in the School of Community book?

The melancholy temperament is defined as positive in as much as it is predisposed to intuit more easily the limits that exist in what seems obvious in things. All things are limited. From the 1700s on, there was the idea that man could resolve everything. And from this prideful presumption – from *rana rupta et bos*, as Aesop said, of the frog that pumped himself up to become like the ox – we passed to the 1900s in which exactly the inverse happened: after the First World War, everyone saw that man is a disaster; and since then, we've only gotten worse. It's only the sure affirmation of an ultimate positivity that allows man to face all problems, to rediscover and to face them again, and to tend towards resolving them until the moment when he has found the solution.

For this reason, people hearing Jesus speak said: "This man – yes, He speaks with authority."[38] What does it mean for a man to speak with authority? A man that speaks knowing what he is saying and having reasons for what he affirms, and with whom you are sure to cross the ford of life. Or else: "No one ever spoke like this man,"[39] because no one gave explanations for life such as that man gave.

There is a melancholy that makes one understand the limits of things, and that, therefore, makes you understand that things are made and sustained by another and it thrusts you into the search for something else; and there's a melancholy, a sadness, that says "Everything is nothing." Like certain people who afterwards, give you a stomach ache, because they come to be consoled by you, and you tell them: "But no, there are also good things," and they say: "No, everything is nothing, nothing is worth anything"; "Then get out and go home!"

Lately, I've been in a relationship with a 27-year-old guy who is sick with a tumour. It's been a provocative relationship, because what he had inside was a desire for life, and, in face of the disease that had already marked his destiny ...
We have, then, a nature that is desire for life, and we have a situation that is going towards death.

He felt that his destiny was contrary to that desire that ...
No! The use of the word "destiny" is wrong! Destiny was for life and the circumstances were for death: destiny wins! Thus, there's immortality; life isn't resolved only in the limits that you have here.

To say "I am sick; I have to die, nevertheless I'd like to live, my destiny would be to live." To say "My destiny would be to live, but I have to die because I have tuberculosis; I have cancer and I have to die" isn't reasoning: it's a psychological giving in, a giving in to a weakness. If your destiny tells you "I am made for life," this means that this is stronger and will prevail, prevail over the fact that you, in the circumstances that you are in, must die. It means that there is something else or another position; if there weren't another position, something else for which destiny triumphs, then all is destined to become nothing. Everything is destined to become nothing: dust inside a tomb, a mummy dried inside a prison for thirty thousand years.

If Christ called us to this path, it's so that we, in the midst of people, may have the ability to carry out this task: shout to everyone the true reason (the true reason is the destiny inherent in our nature) and, therefore, to help people's hope, without which people become violent towards others, lazy in their work (they no longer want to work), and untruthful in front of true things.

The dramatic thing is that 99 per cent of mothers no longer teach these things to their children. Because of this, they're no longer mothers. Mother can also be a filly, if mother means to throw something out from your womb. She is a mother if she educates in destiny. In fact, if a woman adopts a two-month-old baby, a three-month-old, and brings it up teaching it to live and teaching it the value of destiny, the positivity of its life, that woman is truly its mother. Therefore the problem of our vocation is extremely serious, it's the thing the world needs most. In fact, what is the thing which the world needs most? If God were to have become man, He would have done the thing that the world needs most; God became man to say these things, because the world needs these things.

Freedom can allow a total adherence, but also a plain no.
No, and that's it. Bam!

What is the positive side of having freedom? Because I almost want to say that it would be better not to have it.
Go read *The Mystery of the Holy Innocents* by Peguy where God speaks and says how much more beautiful it is to have free men instead of slaves as servants.[40] When He said: "Let

us make man in our image and likeness,"[41] He made man in the image and likeness of what He is, supremely: supreme freedom. God is freedom; freedom is the greatest gift of Himself that God gave man in making him like Himself. For that reason, man is the lord of himself and all creation.

Second: the application of freedom is extremely simple. You have only to recognize and accept the evident, to recognize and to accept, to recognize and to adhere to an evident presence. You collide with the presence: you walk out the door and you collide with your nose against this presence. To recognize and to welcome an evident presence. Therefore, the dynamism of freedom is something extremely simple; here lies its difficulty – that it's simple!

All the hostile fire that tries to scorch freedom is done by flames that say: "But, maybe, if, however," which are all words that don't make you understand reality (the opposite of reason, which is to understand the real), that pull you away from the real, that create a wall of flames to block and impede your path to reality,[42] to use a war-like image. But the term war-like doesn't invoke in us the right image; because the term war-like is a term that in the Bible is a metaphor applied to God, it is a divine term, so much so that the Bible made the presence of God the subject of war to save the Hebrew people, to keep His possession.

An announcement. After Christmas, we'll begin doctors' visits, and I'd like to say a couple of words about this. We who must judge the modality with which you'll proceed on your path in Gruppo Adulto next year, we ask that you have a talk with a doctor, because the path requires that one take it with all of oneself, including one's physical and psychic

aspects. There's only one aim of the visit: that your definitive acceptance into Gruppo Adulto not be against your freedom. That it may be a condition in which you can be free;
free, not suffocated. Is that clear? It's love of your freedom.

3 Obedience

Today we'll take another step in our meditation. What does meditation mean? It means becoming aware of a truth in such a way that it unfolds before your eyes, so that you can penetrate it. It means, therefore, that it isn't a piece of paper nailed to the wall, the wall of your eyes, that is, the wall of your heart, but rather is living words that you can penetrate. We can only penetrate living words, that is, words that are told to us by those whom we live with, those who take part in our life.

1 THE REASONABLE CONSEQUENCE OF FAITH

Up to this point, we've spoken about faith, and about freedom as a condition of faith. Without freedom, there is no faith, just a braying donkey (if you go from behind and prick it with a long darning needle, it will react!). Today, we'll see what virtue faith yields. Faith is an act of knowledge. Freedom is a condition for this to happen. What feeling does this act of knowledge, like every act of knowledge, generate? What type of affectivity does it generate? Affection follows from all acts of knowledge: what kind of affection results from knowledge of faith? Or, in other words, what kind of virtue is the virtue that is proper to faith? What virtue is the virtue proper to faith (where the word "virtue" explains the word affection or affectivity)?

Affection is behaviour. You see a pole and, since you're very weakened from studying, this pole looks like your girlfriend: bad affection results from bad knowledge. Affection is an attitude towards a known object. You thought the pole was a beautiful girl and so you took on a certain attitude, but it went awry! Affection is the attitude towards the known object.

The correct attitude towards a known object, the correct affection borne for a known object is called virtue. To become accustomed to singling out a stanza full of truth and meaning before saying daytime prayer: "to become accustomed to" is called virtue. For example, the virtue of pity. So, virtue is an attitude towards a known object, the correct attitude, normally correct, towards the known object, a habitually correct attitude towards the known object.

I drink because my mouth is dry. But I can also have drunk like this: here's some water, and I drink it. Instead, I'm grateful to Gloria because she brought me water, very kindly. I didn't ask her for it. While I'm drinking, I'm grateful to Gloria because she brought me water. This is a virtue, the virtue of gratitude.

The steps we take should be such that we're not able to turn back. They should be studied, meditated on — which means explained before our eyes — and understood. Therefore, we need to speak about them among ourselves, you

should speak about them among yourselves in such a way
that they are steps that will remain; in other words, so that
the path develops. In this sense, it's better to go slowly,
because someone who goes slowly but surely goes far.

Obedience is born as a reasonable attitude

Do you remember that day[1] when Jesus was followed by a
large crowd – and this is amazing – that forgot to eat, didn't
feel tired, even though it had been almost three days since
they followed Him, so they could hear Him speak? Upon
arriving at the top of the hill, Jesus saw this sea of people
covering the sides of the hill "and had pity on them." It's
those brief notes the gospel points out, particularly on
another occasion,[2] that open up like a window onto the
great panorama of Christ's spirit. "Jesus turned and had pity
on them because they were like sheep without a shepherd."
He had pity on them not only because they were hungry and
tired and continued to follow Him unfazed. His thinking
was broader: why did those people have such a great hunger
and thirst for His word? Because they hadn't ever heard anyone speak like Him, yet the things He said were the things
for which they were born, born of their mothers. They were
born for those things, but no one had ever told them. "And
He had pity on them." This pity was immediately translated
into a realistic acknowledgment: they were hungry. To have
pity on people because they don't know their destiny and
to have pity on people because they're hungry (because for
three days they've been following someone who's speaking

about their destiny), is the same, it's the same gesture. So He told the apostles: "Have them all sit down." They sat and, in the end, He fed them all.

And in those, in those who followed Him to hear Him speak because they were fascinated by that last gesture (even the economic angle was taken care of; they ate without paying), a roar of praise swelled up, and they all began to shout to Christ as the king who was to come, to the king – son of David, descendant of David – who was to come and was to give the whole world over to the Jews, who was to have made the Jewish people the masters of the world: Saviour, but for them "Saviour" and "master" were the same; in the hardness of their hearts, the two things were the same. "Then everyone pressed in," says the gospel, "to make Him king." He escaped from them, and passed furtively to the other side of the lake with the boat. On the other side of the lake was the city of Capernaum, with that beautiful synagogue whose ruins can still be seen today.

The day after was the Sabbath, which He was accustomed to. He entered the world like a man, a man like others. Therefore, just as other men, His contemporaries, went to the synagogue on the Sabbath, He too went to the synagogue, prayed with those in the synagogue, said the psalms we pray and that the Jews have prayed to this day. Whoever wanted to could raise his hand to be called up front to read a part of the Bible, a piece chosen at random, whatever happened to show up on the page, or what was chosen for that day. Jesus always took the occasion to raise His hand and go up and speak. The new things He began to say were put within the context of the old: there was a new way to see the world. The words were the same; there was a new way to see the old words. I'm emphasizing this point, because this is the life of the Christian. This is what it means to be Christian: a newness that always opens up the road within the old words.

That day, the Bible passage was the story of the Hebrews in the desert, whom God fed with manna. And Jesus said: "Your fathers ate manna in the desert, but they died. I will give you manna, I will give you a bread such that whoever eats it will no longer die." Everyone, at the outset, thought that He was speaking metaphorically (metaphor, abstract comparison; if I say: "my words should be like bread for your soul," you know that I'm not talking about bread you eat with your teeth. As bread is food for the body, so words are the bread for the soul). "Your fathers ate manna and then died. My words are like bread: he who eats them, that is, he who assimilates them, will no longer die." The people, I was saying, as strange as it was to them, thought that it was a metaphor, that it was a manner of speaking. But, while He was giving this speech, the door in the back opened and a rush of people entered. They were the same ones from the previous day, some from the previous day, who wanted to make Him king. When He easily and mysteriously fled, they thought: "He must have gone to Capernaum!" So they went all around the lake to get Him, and they entered the synagogue just as He was speaking.

On seeing the people who entered the synagogue, who, tired as they were, without having eaten, couldn't be at peace until they had reached Him again, Jesus (who was a man like other men, like one of us who sees something beautiful and leaps. His heart leapt, and, just as emotion is for us, when the heart leaps, it can give birth to a new image, can give birth to a wonderful idea. This is the way ideas came to Jesus) had the most beautiful idea of His life. He unexpectedly changed the meaning of His words, the meaning of His sermon, and said: "You went looking for me because I fed you with bread, for free. But I will give you something greater to eat. I will give you my flesh to eat and my blood to drink. And whoever eats this bread and drinks this blood will live forever." This time the change of topic, of the meaning of the word bread, was more evident than the first time. Everyone understood that He wasn't speaking through metaphor, wasn't speaking just to speak, but speaking seriously.

Now the leaders – journalists, politicians, university professors, or high-school teachers – those who try to dictate their own conception of life to others, who at that time were called scribes and Pharisees, began to tell the people (they finally had the opening to do it. Before they had waited angrily, but couldn't find an opening): "Did you hear? He's crazy, crazy! Who can give his own flesh to eat, his own blood to drink? He's crazy, crazy!" They spread the idea, the conviction, that He was crazy. And all the people, who always followed like sheep – we should meditate on this, as I said before – all the people repeated the words: "He's crazy, crazy! How is this guy here going to give us His flesh to eat?" And while they said: "He's crazy, crazy!" the Pharisees insisted: "Let's go, let's go; leave Him here, let's go!" Slowly, the people followed the Pharisees and scribes and everyone left the synagogue, so that – it was already evening, it seems that these meetings were always in the afternoon – in the evening twilight, there was a great silence in the synagogue. Jesus was there, looking into space. Imagine how painful this must have been for Him: the supreme moment of man's incomprehension, the symbol of man's incomprehension. But He would understand the supreme moment a little later.

Yet a small group remained: it was a group of *aficionados*, the gang, a gang without weapons, poor things! They were all there with their heads hung, in silence. And Jesus, who, when He said the things He had come for, never gave in, insisted. When the people said: "He's crazy, crazy!" He kept on saying: "If you don't eat my flesh you will not enter the Kingdom of Heaven," which means the truth of things; you will not be saved, you will lose your very selves. He asks those dozen people who remain there in silence, "And you too, do you want to go away?" He doesn't mitigate the inconceivability of what He said, but insists: "And you too, do you want to go away?" As usual, Simon impetuously made himself everyone's spokesman and said: "Master, we don't understand what you say either, but if we go away from you, where shall we go? Only you have the words." The real translation should be, "that correspond to the heart, that give meaning to life." But what does "words that correspond to the heart" mean? Reasonable words! Reason is to understand the correspondence – we at least said this last time – between what somebody says about reality and what the heart expects from reality. Reason is the correspondence between what someone says about life and what needs the heart asks for from life, as *The Religious Sense*[3] says.

Master, if we go away from you where shall we go? Only you have the words that explain life, that give meaning to life; only you have the words that speak of life in a reasonable way, in a way that corresponds to the heart. It should be an easy way, and instead we saw last time that it's the most difficult one. It's the most exceptional way there is: speaking according to the needs of the heart.

Faced with the truly exceptional fact that that man spoke in a way that corresponded to the heart, explained life in a way that corresponded to the heart – therefore it was true – faced with the evidence of the truth in the words that man spoke, faced with this experienced, evident correspondence, this evident correspondence between what He said and the heart – by now they had heard Him speak for months, months and months, and there was an ever greater impression that He was the only one who spoke in a way that corresponded to the heart – what did the people need to do? Was it more logical and reasonable to be scandalized because He said things they didn't understand, or was it more reasonable to say, "I don't understand this, but if I go away from Him no one will speak to me according to my heart? I don't understand this thing, but no one speaks in such a reasonable way as this man does. Therefore I am forced to be loyal toward this man, to be sincere toward this man, that is, to follow this man."

The immediate reaction that one experienced, that a person with a correct position experienced before the question: "Do you also want to go away?" was "We must follow you because you're the only person, the only case that's so exceptional, where a person speaks in a way that always corresponds to the heart. And if now you tell us something different, it means that we don't understand it, for now. You'll explain it to us. We'll understand it tomorrow, but we can't leave you just because we don't understand these words." And even regarding the words they didn't understand, such as "I will give you my flesh to eat," they couldn't say, "This is insane!" They could only say, "Who knows what it means!" The reasonable attitude was, "Who knows what it means!"

With regard to the rest, there is some evidence to add: those people in the synagogue, who came because they'd been fed for free the day before and who, instigated by the Pharisees, went away, were unreasonable. Why? For the simple reason that now He said something incomprehensible, truly incomprehensible – you couldn't say against the heart, but incomprehensible, yes – they went away, they were unreasonable. Because they did something that contradicted what they had seen the day before. The day before they had followed Him because He had given out bread. To go away because they didn't understand was to negate the evidence of the day before. They saw something the day before, something so affecting that they returned to look for it again. Since they didn't understand what they heard Him say, since it was incomprehensible, they went away and left Him, saying: "He's crazy!" Fine, He might be crazy, or perhaps you're the one who's crazy because the day before He made you go there to look for Him! The most evident thing is that you were crazy the day before. But they hadn't reasoned like that: it was evident that what they had done the day before was right. They didn't reproach themselves for having gone after Him without having eaten yet another day. What He had done the day before was too evident.

Thus, before the exceptional fact of that man who always speaks in a way that corresponds to the heart, as no one else ever had, the most immediate and logical consequence is to follow. As Saint Peter said: "If we go away from you, where shall we go? There is no other meaning left in life. Only you have the words that explain life, the words that correspond to the heart." And, in fact, whoever went away contradicted themselves, went away contradicting themselves.

Summing up, for the first time we've seen a fact in the gospel in which the correct conclusion to the event was the one of the apostles who, like all the other people, had seen what Jesus had done and said for months. And everyone said, "Truly a prophet has risen up. It's miraculous. He's the only one who speaks like that. This man here is the only one who really speaks with authority," because what He said corresponded to their hearts. But at a certain point, faced with one of his incomprehensible expressions, incomprehensible to them, they gave in to public opinion, to the equivalent of the newspapers and television and the politicians. They said: "He's crazy!" because He said something that was outside their normal mental sphere. Not that it was against the heart: it was incomprehensible. The right thing to have done is what Peter and his other friends did: they followed Him just the same. "We may not understand, nevertheless no one speaks according to the human heart as you do, so if we go away from you where shall we go? Life would have no more meaning." Therefore they followed Him. These were the reasonable ones. Simon was reasonable, the apostles who remained there were reasonable – puzzled, because even they didn't understand, but reasonable. They followed Him all the same: this is the beginning of an affective attitude. The others went away refusing Him, regardless of what they had seen and heard. This little group remained, adhering to Him, following Him. It's the beginning of the concept of obedience that is born of reason, or better, born as a reasonable attitude. "Who speaks like you? Without you, life would have no meaning, only you know how to give meaning to life." So it is a favourable attitude towards Him, an attitude of adhesion to Him, which in that moment was put to the test. But it was right to follow Him, since otherwise they would have had to negate all the preceding months when they were with Him, in which it became clear to them that that man was a man different from the rest.

The content of the word "follow"

The second thing. Can we explain or specify better the content of the word *follow*, of this affective adherence that Simon and the others had, the reason they were with Him? They were with Him. Watch out: not on His side; you can't only say "on His side," as if they had approved of what He said. They didn't say, "We approve of what you say" – because they didn't understand well either – but "with Him" yes. They followed Him, adhered to Him, regardless of the fact that they didn't understand. Is it clear? They followed Him. Is there anything that explains better this following Him that Simon and the other eleven understood in that moment of crisis or trial?

Here you don't have to look further at John 6, but rather at the letter of Saint Paul to the Philippians, where it says: "Have in yourselves the same feeling Christ had towards the Father."[4] Have the same feelings in yourselves toward Christ that Christ had towards the Father. To follow Christ means to have the same feelings as Christ, the same feelings Christ had towards the Father. To follow Christ means to assimilate, to assume, the same attitude that Christ had towards the Father. For Christ it was evident that the Father was God of Heaven and earth. Because Christ was a man. "How should we pray?" "Our Father, who art in Heaven, your kingdom come ..." He taught them this way.

We must have towards Christ the same attitude Christ had towards the Father. For Christ it was evident that everything belonged to the Father. And when the Father permitted Him to be killed? "Father, if it's possible don't let me be killed, but not my will but yours be done." For Christ it was evident that God was everything, therefore He needed to adhere to the Father even when the Father's attitude was incomprehensible for Him. Christ, even when the Father permitted Him to be killed, which was an unjust thing, and Christ, as man, didn't understand why, so much so that He prayed, "Father, if it's possible, don't let me die." You can't go against the Father. For all the evidence you might otherwise have, without the Father there is no meaning in life − He adhered to the Father, followed the Father. So man must have the same attitude towards Christ that Christ had towards the Father. Christ says something incomprehensible, but if we negate this, we negate everything, there isn't anything left. So it's right to adhere to Christ. To follow Christ means having the same feeling towards Christ that Christ had towards the Father, towards the mystery of God.

What word can we use to define the attitude Christ had towards the Father? It's what Saint Paul says some lines after: "was obedient even unto death." Simon and the others became obedient to Christ even before the incomprehensible. Just as the attitude of Christ towards the Father was obedience even when the Father decided to let Him die, so even for us, the attitude we should have towards Christ is the same: obedience to Christ even when we find ourselves before something we don't understand.

Therefore to follow Christ, explained in the most precise way, means to have the same feelings that Christ, as a man, had towards God. We too must have the same attitude towards Christ that He had towards the mystery of God: the attitude of adhesion, of obedience. Obedience defines the attitude of Christ before the Father. Christ recognizes, accepts, and adheres to the plan of the Father, so that even when the Father's plan implied His death, Christ recognizes that that's the road of His life. The obedience to the Father is, for Christ, as a man, following the Father. The same feeling should be in us towards Him: to follow Christ, to obey Christ.

As an assignment, you will read the fifth through the eighth chapters of Saint John's gospel, looking for all the sentences in these four chapters that demonstrate following, demonstrate obedience; all the sentences that show that Christ was obedient to the Father. For example: "I always do the will of my Father." And copy all the sentences into your notebooks: in-class assignment! The class is the world, the door of this class is the final judgment. We leave this class with the sheet of paper with these sentences written on it; it will be a part of the exam!

Because of this God glorified Him

It says in Saint Paul's letter to the Philippians, second chapter, which is important and which I have already cited: "For this God glorified Him." He followed the Father, so the Father glorified Him, exalted Him. "You have obeyed, and I accomplish what your heart was made for, your heart was made to be the Saviour of the universe, of the world." And He gave everything over to Him. Saint Paul also says, "He gave everything into His hands."

This is analogous to what Jesus says in Saint John's gospel, "He who obeys me will do the things I have done, will do the miracles I have done, and greater things than these," because the evidence of the strength of Christ is much stronger now. In this world that is entirely against Him, the strength of Christ is stronger now, in His Church, greater than even two thousand years ago. Two thousand years ago He performed some miracles, now He performs miracles galore. The value of Christ and His body is demonstrated in a much greater way now, mysteriously but visibly, than it was two thousand years ago.

As a second part of your assignment: read chapters 14–17 of Saint John attentively, looking for the sentences. But, before starting to read the gospel, say a *Glory be* to the Spirit, from whom man's reason and intelligence according to his total capacity – and thus according to the acuteness of faith – originates. This is because faith is the apex of human knowledge, the apex of reason's knowledge. This is a gift we receive, the gift of partaking in the Spirit with which Christ possesses the world and "every living thing."[5]

The reasonableness of following

Precisely because Christ was obedient unto death God exalted Him and gave Him a name above all other names. This is the exaltation of our lives, too. Our lives, if we obey, become greater than they could have ever been, that is, they are fulfilled.[6]

For us, obedience – that is, following the design of Another, doing His will – is only reasonable in one instance: you must be aware that the success of life lies in this. You can be in a convent for decades without having this awareness. So you live poorly, since one cannot live one's dedication to the Lord without the awareness that this in itself fulfills life more than would have happened had one done what one liked, felt, and imagined. The gospel expresses this concept like this: "He who follows me will have eternal life and a hundredfold here below." The hundredfold is true fulfillment, that already begins in this world, and is completed in eternity.

Merry Christmas to everyone! On Christmas night ask the Lord for the grace to make your life a witness to Him, because the witness to God made man ... have I ever told you about Manfredini? About Monsignor Manfredini, Bishop of Bologna, one of the greatest bishops in this impoverished clerical season? One time we were going to church at night, we were hurrying down the steps because we were late, and Manfredini ran up next to me and grabbed my arm. So I said to him: "What do you want?" "Just think: the fact that God was made man, was born as a man ..." He took a step in front of me, then he turned around, "it's something that is out of this world!" And I told him seriously, "Yes, it really is something that is out of this world ... in this world."

What instrument do you use to understand that it's like this? The lives of those called to this, the witness of our lives that are changed by faith. Therefore at Christmas we need to ask Christ that, having begun the good work in us, He bring it to completion. And what is the good work, the great good work, the greatest value in the world? Witnessing to Christ. If you get rid of this, you get rid of the meaning of everything that happens, you get rid of the meaning of the world. So the world becomes an empty desert, as Eliot says.[7]

2   TRUE OBEDIENCE IS A FRIENDSHIP

Following someone who is in front of you

Following means to look at someone who's before you. What's the first characteristic, the fundamental characteristic of someone before you? The person who's before you is the visage of what you have encountered and what first nudged you, gave you an idea, a desire. From the exterior point of view, it was someone, it was the encounter with someone (with a classmate, with a priest ...) or with some people in a context (in a church, on a street, in a class at school, at work) that made you say, without even realizing it, "Look how different this guy is!" This person made you take note of a difference, a human difference that had, as a characteristic, that of corresponding more sharply, more deeply to the heart in its simplicity. It was a human difference, a difference in living the human life that you acknowledged – confusedly, more or less confusedly, but you acknowledged it – to the extent that the way of living that this guy or those other guys had corresponded to the needs of your heart in a way that was different from usual. It was inclusive, and was, therefore, an ideal. It brought out or provoked an ideal image that had never been brought out before by the way others lived.

More particularly, there was a characteristic that you didn't stop to reflect on, but that you now must stop and reflect on: that man, those people, those classmates ... that difference first of all implied a seriousness in living. Life, for that person, was a serious thing. It implied a seriousness in living that carried with it a taste for living, a desire to do things, a usefulness in relationships, a goodness.

Normally in life, the problem of money is serious for everyone, the problem of children is serious, the problem of man and woman is serious, the problems of health and politics are serious: for the world, everything is serious except life. I don't mean life – life as health is a serious thing, certainly – but *life*. Yet what is more *life* than health, money, the relationship between a man and a woman, children, work? What more is life than this? What does it involve? Life involves all these things, but with a goal for everything, with a meaning. You were struck by a way of living that heralded, that brought with it – it isn't that you were told all these things, but, thinking it over, you should find all these things within your own beginning! – that bore with it the affirmation of the meaning of life. Life is a serious thing with meaning. It's a serious thing. Therefore it's a task before the whole world, before all creation, before all times, before history, before time and space, and it's an ultimate, definitive, complete meaning.

Following: to understand and imitate

So how does watching someone before you become following? If you imitate him. You must watch the person before you and imitate him. What does it mean to imitate him? It means two things: first of all, it means to understand what the person says, to understand the steps he takes. Man's steps are translated into thoughts, words, judgments ... Therefore, to understand thoughts, to understand what the person says, and then, to imitate him in the way he does things.

If you stop at the first step, that is, at only hearing the words, you won't follow him. You also have to try to be attentive to how he does things and try to do them as he does. This is why not all wordmongers are teachers, because to be a teacher you have to show how it's done, too. More precisely, to be a teacher is to use words such that you make *how* to use them understood by the very way you use them.

To understand things someone says requires the least amount of effort imaginable. It requires simplicity, requires having the heart of a child. And to be attentive to how a person does things also requires the curiosity of a child.

There's a word we use to indicate all this. We say that the rule of life is to follow. If you don't like the word (as I don't), you can get rid of it. What matters is that you retain the concept. The concept implies: first, something you have before you; second, something from which we try to understand the words; and third, something from which we try to understand how the words are carried out, are lived. The whole thing is called following. Without following, without the intensity of following, our life has nothing before it, doesn't know what to think, doesn't know how to do things. Therefore it identifies whatever pops into its head (the reaction to its own opinions) as its own thought and identifies doing whatever it feels like, whatever pleases it, as a rule of action (which means it's ruled by instinctiveness). The alternative to life as following is instinctiveness, which means to degrade man to the level of animal. (Well, for these insights you have to have a heart that is so simple that it's already very wise. You need a lot of wisdom to understand these things!)

Obedience, gesture of the I

To follow, then, implies trying to understand what you're told. What does it mean to understand? Understanding is an act of reason, it's a verb that refers to reason, it's reason's way of living. What does understanding as reason's way of living mean? It means to light upon, to grasp, to make evident to yourself (or at least to glimpse) the correspondence between what you're told and what you are (and the needs of your heart, that is, the needs of your life, the profound needs of your I). To understand means to grasp the profound correspondence between what you're told and your I, the needs of your I, the profound needs of your heart, the profound needs of your life.

Therefore following isn't something I can put on like an overcoat (I'm dressed, more or less, and I grab an overcoat and put it on). No, it's not an overcoat like the concept of obedience that you find around, where to obey means to say yes, to do what they tell you. No sir! Obeying begins as effort and work. (Take heed, because it's a question of simplicity of heart, thus of recognizing the evidence of a correspondence between what you're told and the needs of your heart, of your life.) What you're told is out of love for your life, and should be heeded! What you're told makes your taste for life increase, makes all of your life become truer. To be able to say "I" consciously, with an ever greater dignity – said *The Journeying*[8] – you have to really listen to what you're told and try to understand.

Bit by bit as you begin to understand, you no longer depend on who says it to you. Bit by bit as it's said to you, it's as if the one who told you has become one with you yourself. You follow yourself. At its limit, the extreme form of obedience is following the discovery of yourself operating in the light of the words and example of another, without which you fumbled in the dark, or lived like an animal.

It's because it corresponds to you that I say: "Do this, pay attention to this other person." I say it to you out of love for your life. And you know what makes me capable of saying it to you out of love for your life? Love for my own life. It's because I've taken my own life seriously that I tell you,

"Look, please, because this is important for your life. If you follow me, you'll understand. And then, after, you'll follow yourself. Following me is like following yourself, we're friends."

True following is friendship

This is friendship. Real obedience is when it reaches this level of friendship. Otherwise it isn't obedience, it's slavery, it's something childish and "yes ma'am" (with the rod even!). Then, if you try to understand, it becomes easier and easier, and becomes more of a desire to understand how I live what I'm letting you understand, or how whoever's before you lives what he or she tells you. "How can I live this?" you say, without saying it to him or her. Following who is before you means asking: "How can you live this? How does one live this?" Understand that here, the principal accent is on desire, the desire to live that we also have, the desire to live. The seriousness in living, the truth in living, and the desire to live. It's the desire to live that makes you ask: "How do you manage to do it, how do you fulfill what you understand?"

Do you understand why I said before that true obedience is a friendship? Because, if I make you understand that what I'm telling you, I'm telling you because it corresponds to the needs of your heart, you'll say: "Thanks for telling me that! Thanks for telling me that!" and this becomes yours, and you have to follow yourself. This is following your own conscience. Your own, true conscience is really the very conscience that's made great and mature by an encounter. And this makes people friends.

If you're friends, then you understand more. If you place everything in the light of friendship, you understand that you have more desire, you understand more that you have the desire to ask, "What about you? How do you do this, how do you carry out these things?" And the other tells you, "I don't know how to explain it to you, watch me!" Or, "Come with me!" Or, "Start to do it like this. For example, fix yourself on the moment during the day in which you say 'God,' but say it stopping and thinking about the word you're saying. Or, because it can be too abstract that way, say: 'Come, Lord.' This is already more readily full of feeling. Say it three times a day. Or: Three times during the day, stop for two minutes to think about the moment in which God became a clot of blood in the body of a woman, the *Angelus*." Or I might tell you, "Sing a song, such as *Povera Voce* or *Mi Prendi Per La Mano*. Sing this song, but give weight to the words, be attentive to the words." Or I'll tell you: "Every night say a Hail Mary to understand the things you don't understand, and also to understand how to do things, because I don't know what else to tell you. Just watch how I do things." Or: "If you don't understand what I'm doing, ask me about it. That way it's easier for me to respond to you, I'll explain it better. Because otherwise, it becomes theoretical. If you ask me how to do things, I'll answer you in a theoretical way. But if you tell me, 'Why did you do it like that?' then I'll be more concrete, more practical."

Listen, friendship unfolds like that. This is friendship. Therefore, true following is friendship, true obedience is friendship. What is called obedience is really friendship, and in fact Saint Paul, speaking of Jesus, said that lov-

ing the Father (He who was in front of Him, before Him),
He became obedient unto death,[9] right to the end. He had
understood that what the Father wanted from Him was
right (it was right out of pity for man, to be able to save man,
to be able to give man freedom, to be able to bring man to
happiness) and He could not *not* do it because His divine
nature could not say no (He was man, thus obedient, but His
person, His I, that was of the Father's substance, His divine
heart was an impetus of love, because "God is love," as Saint
John said[10]). He understood what the Father asked of Him
and knew how to do it. He imitated the Father who had created the world for love.

Synthesis

Anyway, I wanted to say that the word obedience is iden-
tical to the word friendship. A friendship that isn't obedience is a sentimental thing, without fruit or history, without
aim or duration, without a face. The face is given by something that came before you and moved you. And then you
began to try to understand the words, and to understand the
words (to begin to understand means to begin to see how
much they correspond to your heart), and now it's almost
second nature to ask, "And how do you do it, afterwards?"
And that person told you, "Listen, you have to follow me,
watch what I do. Keep following me." Now, really, sym-
biosis happens between what happened to me and my life.
It happens as a oneness, an ever deeper oneness. This is what
they call friendship. This is why the Bible says, "He who
finds a friend truly finds a treasure,"[11] finds the richness of
life. So what characterizes a friend? A friend is character-

ized first and above all by seriousness towards life, by the affirmation that life is a serious thing. Life is a serious thing: serious before the universe (thus it has a task) and serious before destiny (thus it has an ultimate meaning that must be reached). Nothing corresponds to your heart more than these two things.

And then there are many other things that you understand, that correspond, and so you ask, "How do you approach your destiny?" And as I am the one here before you, I tell you. But I know that I'm explaining it badly, so I say to you, "Come back tomorrow, OK? Because tomorrow I'll try to tell you in a better way, and the day after tomorrow I'll try to tell you in an even better way, and then, finally, we'll need to tell it to each other every day, because that way, we'll say it to each other better. And after many, many, many days, it becomes like something that's flowing, like looking each other in the eye. We look each other in the eye and we understand. We understand how to do it. The desire to do it comes. The desire to do it actually comes. And one is no longer alone. One is finally oneself, because one is together. And, in fact, man's I is destined to be united with everything there is, to the mystery of Being. Why? Because man was made in the image of God and God is a communion: the communion of the Father, the Son, and the Spirit, the mystery of the Trinity. The root of the fact that the I is not alone is in the mystery of the Trinity. An I that is alone is an I that is lost. So the I that is not alone is created in a companionship, by a companionship that is friendship. And friendship is created by obedience.

The word obedience is nothing other than the virtue of friendship.

Our meeting today is of great importance as an evaluation and judgment of what we have heard up to now. But above all it has great importance in terms of the work that you must set up to develop and clarify ever more what we've told you.

You haven't, or you have only partially, understood what we've told you up till now; some more, some less, some very little, and some nothing. But it doesn't matter because the Lord put us together so that we might walk together. And to walk means to understand, above all to understand the relationship – between the moment that passes and is gone in an instant, between things that are, yet after a little while, are no longer; to understand the relationships we have which, after a while, show themselves to be different from what we thought – the relationship between the instant and the destiny of the instant.

For someone who walks, what is a step? The relationship between what I'm doing now and my final destiny. This relationship establishes the value of what I'm doing now, so that through what I'm doing now, I understand what destiny is.

However, today's dialogue is important. I'd like to insist on repeating this, but if I insist, we won't have any more time for the assembly! We have so little time, that it will just be an example for you of work that you must carry on. You must carry on with what has been told you up to today, so that when you hear faith or obedience spoken about, for example, you'll be able to understand the words more completely, according to their meaning.

This is an important time, and it has two points of view. First, a general point of view from October up to now, thereby clarifying the goal of the journey that we've taken in these three months. Second, something particular may have struck us, or else something we didn't understand, or something that we like a lot. In clarifying the particular, the total subject is necessarily clarified. To clarify the particular, you necessarily have to be called back to the total subject and, therefore, to the destiny of our journeying.

For example, in the early years, when I used to have discussions in high-school class, one of my favourite subjects to use for an attack was hell: "Horror, horror! How can you say that hell exists? It's disgraceful, unfair, and inconceivable for man." What did I have to do to respond to this objection, which was a specific objection? To respond, I had to trace the specific objection back to the ultimate destiny of man, the ultimate idea of man. The ultimate idea of man is that man is a freedom, that is, something made for happiness. Paradoxically, this is where hell is born. Without hell, there wouldn't be freedom, without the possibility of hell, there wouldn't be freedom. Why? Because freedom involves the possibility to say no, and to say no is hell. Hell is a big no. Therefore, hell – paradoxically – becomes the word that most indicates man's dignity. Not because hell may be beautiful, but because – as I have already said–it affirms man as freedom. That is to say, in a positive sense, that a happiness to which I didn't say yes can't be mine. If I were not to say yes, the happiness that I reach wouldn't be mine. For it to be mine, I must choose it, I must want it, it must be an object of my freedom.

Let's begin, then! We can begin with the details, or we can ask for information on some passage that you didn't understand, on an idea that remained murky. If possible, we should leave today without having left any important scraps behind.

When obedience was being discussed, it was said that the greatest work that is needed is simplicity of heart ...

For instance, *work* would be the wrong word. You understand the intention, but it is the wrong word. Simplicity of heart is a *condition* for obedience.

I thought that simplicity of heart, deep down, is needed to understand all the steps taken up to now.

Jesus is of your opinion. In the eleventh chapter of the gospel of Saint Matthew, he thanks the Father, because He made known the right things to the simple of heart and not to those who think they already know.[12] Therefore, what you say is right: simplicity is a condition for everything that we have heard said.

But, of all that we have heard said, the phenomenon that simplicity is most important for – if we can define a hierarchy – is obedience, because in obedience you really need to be simple, otherwise it's useless.

Faith proposes and assures something incredibly beautiful, so beautiful that it becomes almost easy to say yes. But it's not the case with obedience. In obedience, you always have to follow something else and not yourself. Freedom is beautiful this way. It has its own unmistakable flavour. So, to affirm one's own freedom with simplicity can be even easier than saying yes and following on life's path, as a criterion of the path, what another says. Therefore, simplicity is needed for everything, but above all, for obedience.

In the lesson on faith, you told us that only the moral I, the united I is capable of trusting ...

Wait a minute: what does the moral I, the united I, mean? What is the moral I? The true I! What is the united I? It's the undivided I, therefore it's the true I. So: only the true I is capable of trusting.

Then, how can one live obedience so that in everyday life, in front of daily decisions, I can decide without asking every moment, without asking someone else about every responsibility?

So, problem: how to live your own freedom every day, your own I, in such a way that you are not forced to run to "mama," to run to whomever the guide is, to say, "What am I supposed to do?"

Answer: the more that you have made the criteria of the person who guides you your own, the more you have understood and accepted the criteria that were offered, the more you are free from going to ask during the course of the day. To accept the principles that they gave you, to accept the laws that they have indicated for you, means that you are truly free, without needing to run and ask someone or another's opinion. Therefore, those who accept not their own criteria but the criteria of the person guiding them are free. That is, they are truly themselves, they truly affirm their own dignity. Accepting the criteria of the person who guides you is the way to be free in everything that you do. You become wise in everything that you do, you know how to act. It's what Jesus said, "Whoever loses himself, finds himself."[13] Whoever gives up his or her own point of view to follow Jesus, to follow Him, becomes a person capable of facing anything, a person who knows what he or she is doing, who makes the right decisions.

The Bible uses different words, "Vir oboediens loquetur victoriam."[14] Those who follow the criteria of the person who guides them, of the authority, therefore those who follow the criteria of God – those who follow the criteria of the other who guides them in the name of God – will act well in front of any circumstance. They will face the circumstance well, in a way that's useful for their own lives.

This is why I said that to be able to respond – as we're doing – to all of the details that you can raise as objections or questions, we will be forced to recall always the ultimate principles that they gave us. Following those principles, we understand all the details.

Since it seems to me that obedience is an affective matter, I would like you to explain further the two aspects of obedience: "to understand the steps of the person who is ahead" and "to imitate how they take them." In particular, I would like to understand whether these two things are what allow affective adherence.

You said something wrong in principle and you corrected it at the end, saying the opposite. The opposite is true, that is, affective attachment is born from following another. And, in fact, God, in His wisdom, said, "You don't know how to reach me. I will come to trace the path. Whoever follows me – I am the way – will find truth and life."[15]

The attachment to Jesus is born precisely from the attitude of attention, from the fixed gaze, from the question to understand, from the adherence to what they tell you to do. Affection is born from here, and it isn't true that you need affection to be able to follow. Suppose you have affection for a person and she tells you something contrary to another thing that you care about. Let's say you have affection for A and hold to one of your criteria. If the person you have affection for asks you something contrary to what you hold, most likely you will lose trust in this person and will detach yourself from her to follow your own ideas. Instead, the opposite is true: if you adhere to the indication that the other person gives you, that the authority gives you, if you try to understand her, you will discover the truth and life more than before and this makes you admire the other and makes you affectionate towards the other. To understand this means to begin to understand how our companionship is born, how a community is born, how friendship is born.

The true companionship, meaning a constructive, creative factor of life, and therefore generator of beauty, consolation – repairing what falls down – a positive companionship in this sense can be born only from a friendship. Friendship is the virtue, the energy that constructs the companionship. This is why the Lord, wanting man to know Him, became man and this man generated a companionship. He became present here and now, in every moment of history, within a companionship. And if one claims to have a relationship with the mystery of God and leaves out the companionship, and, in particular, leaves out an authority that guides it, one deceives oneself; it would be an illusion.

In fact, many people in the Movement have entered the cloister. Why do all those who leave – and there are many of them – do so? The big difficulty is not the silence or loneliness (because man has to die. The cloister is like beginning to live the awareness that death is where everyone ends up). They leave because of their incapacity to carry the community within themselves. Inversely, when people ask me whether they should enter the cloistered convent, the criterion that I have always used is how they live the community. How do they conceive of and live the companionship? If they do not live the companionship or the community as a necessary friendship, it's useless for them to ask me to enter the convent. I would tell them right away that they are taking the wrong path.

So what is friendship? Friendship, in its minimal state, is the encounter of one person with another person whose destiny he or she desires more than his or her own life: I desire your destiny more than I desire my life. The other reciprocates this and desires my destiny more than his or her life. Friendship is like this, and the proof that this is true is that you'd want anyone you meet in the diversity of circumstances to understand this, so that everyone would embrace each other. Those who do not experience this must humbly ask the Lord and the Blessed Mother to make it understood to them, because without this, not even the relationship with God is true.

If I desire your destiny and you desire my destiny, ours is a companionship, the primary companionship, a companionship in its minimal state. But if I live this, I desire that anyone I meet participate in it. Then, you and I, who met each other first, want to pull the others we meet into our friendship too, so that there are seven of us, then twenty. Then we'll want everyone on the subway to take part in our companionship, and there are two hundred people on the subway. We'd like all of the two hundred people to become part of the companionship. This way, you can even make a house with two hundred people. And you'll see how beautiful that house is, because everything goes on according to a scale fixed by the Lord. There's the first person you met, who is like the first point of reference; then the second, the third, the fourth, the fifth, the sixth, the seventh, the eighth, and then, the two hundredth: the hierarchy of affections remains as God brought it about in you.

But the more you have affection, the more you're tempted to stop there, to grab, to possess. That's the way you lose both the thing and yourself: you lose. The symptom that a friendship is wrong is that the others are extraneous. Do you remember the poetry of Pär Lagerkvist that I read at the university retreat?[16] He says to her: everything else doesn't exist. Only you and I exist. It is egoism assembled into a system. And not only is this deadly, it's suffocating (the third day, I can't take it any more. I need some air. I need to see a horse galloping!).

I was struck when I read about the friendship between you and Manfredini: "... between us, we said 'the Church has to revive, the Christian reality has to be more self-aware.' We were in the third year of high school, but the question could arise because we were already at a certain depth of friendship." [17]

I remember the very moment during an outing when we were passing under the bridge of a train that goes by Meda, between Meda and Seveso. I still remember it – Manfredini was in the third year of high school, so I was thirteen years old – I still remember the place where we were talking when he said these things.

I thought, "So friendship isn't an option. It's almost a necessity for an understanding of myself and of reality."

The word that clears up the whole question is the word *option*. Friendship is not an *option*. If it's an *option*, it's not friendship. Friendship is not something you can or cannot have. Without friendship one is no longer oneself. This is so true that when God created man, He said, "Man cannot be alone. He needs a companion." [18] And so He created the first companionship, which is the companionship between man and woman (between man and woman, because there were tasks to complete as well).

In what sense is friendship not an *option*, but necessary? That is, one can't have it or not have it? If one does not have friendship, he's not even a man. He's not himself, he's wounded, he can't but be sad. You wouldn't even trust him to keep five cents for you. You can't trust him. In what sense is friendship necessary?

Because friendship is "a companionship guided to destiny."
This is a clear example that one can repeat a phrase without grasping where it came from, without being aware of how it's born. It's true that friendship is a companionship guided to destiny. But guided by whom? If there are two of you, who's leading? Something else, a third party, is needed.

And this is the third party because you meet him or her at the second step instead of the first? No! This thing you follow is something inherent to the person you're together with and is something so beautiful that it makes you come together. It's so right that it makes you get together. If it's so right and beautiful that it makes you get together, it immediately produces, it generates. "The barren woman will become the mother of many sons,"[19] and man, Abraham, "will become father of many peoples."[20] If your being together is something beautiful and true, you'd like whoever you meet to know that beauty, to know that goodness, to know that justice. And so you tell him or her, "Come and have a beer," and so instead of two, there are three of you. And later, instead of three, you number thirty, and then after that, there are three thousand of you, and then after that, a hundred thousand. There were four of those first guys that I met at Berchet, and right away they became three, because one died. There weren't a hundred thousand of them ...

Whoever really lives the movement – now I'm talking about the Movement, let alone *Memores Domini* – and goes, for example – let's talk about an example that's happening right now – to Formosa, and upon meeting some people tells them why he's with a particular group of people. This is an incredibly right and beautiful friendship. Beyond this nothing is right or beautiful. Something may appear to you as right and beautiful, but after a little while, if you ask yourself, "and then?" ... it's over. It can't be sustained.

This is why the Jews used the same root word to say *futile* (that which passes, the ephemeral), *falsehood* (because what is ephemeral, that is, what passes, is deceitful), and *man* (because he passes). The same root word indicates man, falsehood, and the ephemeral.

Why did I become such a great friend of Manfredini and DePonti, whom I was always with? From third year of high school to fourth year of theology we were always together – always, I mean always! – and nobody ever said anything because the great reason that we were together was so evident to everyone. In fact, anyone who showed up, at any moment of the day or week, would have heard us speaking about certain things, so much so that a lot of people said, "Oh brother, not those guys again!" and they left. The same people who left other things! Why did we, who didn't even know each other, become such close friends? Because we began to intuit and to speak about certain things, things apart from which life was not worth living. This was the depth that God gave us the grace to have at thirteen or fourteen years old: to understand that apart from certain things, in other words, from Christ, life was not worth living in the literal sense of the term. Everything would become a political game, as justice is today. Everything would become violence, as politics is today. They're all the opposite of what they should be! And the remedy for this is absolutely not speaking about morals and values, as many of our superiors do. Rather, the remedy is to create, to show everyone, to make everyone see, that a companionship that exists because of the encounter with Christ, a companionship that's created because people have encountered Christ, makes one realize that all politics, all culture, and everything else, aren't things that make life worth living.

And so we three were the greatest friends among everyone because our relationship was born from an interest much deeper than what everyone else was interested in. Otherwise, it isn't a companionship. Otherwise, friendship is what everyone says or what I called Utopia this year. What can help us bear all the evil that exists in life so that we can go on? Companionship is like this now. But that companionship is not our companionship.[21] Authentic companionship is what is born when one meets someone else who has seen something just, beautiful, and true and tells him or her about it. And since this person also desires justice, beauty, and truth, they get together. And this person begins to be interested whomever he or she meets, everyone , in order to tell them about justice, beauty, and truth. This way a companionship is born and expands. This is the true monastery. The first Christians and the Middle Ages converted the world in this way, by creating this companionship. It was intolerable for Manfredini, for my classmate and for me, to get in line to go on the outings that the seminarians went on and to speak about something else. It was intolerable! Rather, it was better to be quiet, to shut up.

This friendship gives birth to affection, gave birth to affection. And affection is like the cement of companionship. In this cement, the companionship grows and becomes an edifice, the temple of God in this world, this world to which God would be unknown.

The opposite of a companionship that is born like this is an egoism full of illusion, an egotistical illusion, an egocentric illusion, which means a position that seeks relief in one's own thoughts. And this is against reason. Why is looking for satisfaction in one's own thoughts against reason? Because reason is awareness of reality, not awareness of your thoughts separated from a reference to the real. Reason is awareness of a reality! Reason makes you intuit the presence of the ideal and makes you pursue the ideal. The alternative to the ideal, following your thoughts, is called dreaming. The ideal is the reality that you conquer piece by piece, step by step, while the dream vanishes; it mutates and vanishes from one day to the next.

What does it mean that each one of you had the vocation to virginity? Each one of you had the vocation from God, from Christ – from Christ, because Christ is the one who chooses men to follow Him. "The Father has given everything over to Him."[22] It is a man who is God, but He is a man! The vocation: Christ chose you as instruments to tell others what He is, to awaken in others the love for what He is. Because He is the destiny of everyone. Yet you will awaken the love of Christ in others through your presence, your loving of Christ, your presence that loves Christ, who is the destiny of everyone. It is only through a presence that it is communicated to others. The human presence in the world, in all its possible factors, according to all the factors of which it is made, is called companionship or community.

CONCLUSION: FROM FAITH TO OBEDIENCE

Faith

How did you do with faith? What phenomenon is faith? It's a phenomenon of knowledge. If it is a phenomenon of knowledge, it involves reason. It's not that it is "reduced" to reason, but it involves it.

Therefore a phenomenon of knowledge that involves reason is a phenomenon of knowledge of what exists, of reality. And since what faith says, in the reality that our reason measures and understands, doesn't exist – and, in fact, we said that faith is knowledge of a reality that is beyond, of a reality that is *more* than what reason knows – how can you admit this, this *more* than what reason knows? Because our heart only senses the answer to what it is in the face of a hypothesis, at the announcement, at the intuition of this *more*. This way, faith is the most rational thing that exists, because it fulfills reason, that is to say, it finally responds to what the heart desires. It indicates the existence of the reality that fulfills what the heart desires. And this reality is something greater than the fig tree and blackberry bush of Angiolo Silvio Novaro's poetry, "on the fig tree and on the blackberry bush / adorned with golden gems."[23] It's something present in us that determines the existence of something that is beyond us! This is why faith is the supremely reasonable gesture. Without it, reason wouldn't even be possible. It wouldn't be possible to affirm what man moves for.

Therefore, of all we have said thus far, the great word is the word "faith," because this takes in everything, it affirms the world's newness. The newness of the world is the possibility of an encounter in which man perceives that the answer to his heart, to the needs of his heart, exists. This answer – that exists, that is what his heart desires – influences the present, it's already in the present.

When John and Andrew found Christ, they didn't understand the beyond, what paradise could mean, but they felt something there that was like a paradise, a piece of paradise: it was a piece of something Other. It already exists, it's something present. Therefore, faith is to grasp, to recognize a present, to recognize that already in the present, something is beginning that, notwithstanding everything, awaits us. Something already exists in the present that belongs to destiny, that has the form of destiny. Here, here's the more beautiful word: the encounter with a present in whose form destiny already exists.

Freedom

To recognize this, that is, to have faith, to affirm faith, is freedom. The first thing that belongs to destiny that man finds in faith is precisely freedom. Freedom is the need for total satisfaction. Freedom is the capacity to adhere to destiny, the need for the totality of the answer.

Because of this, you can see that freedom that doesn't adhere, that says "no," that resists what faith says, is meaninglessness, is negativity. It's premature death (as the medieval fathers called sin: premature death). Death is a "no" to life.

In fact, if freedom doesn't adhere to faith, all of the terms of relationships are altered. The example that we must always use is that of the affection between man and woman, because this is the example that God first placed in the world. The relationship between man and woman is altered. It becomes egoism instead of love, negation instead of affirmation, arid fragility instead of fruitful creativity, closedness instead of openness. Instead of throwing its arms wide open to embrace the world, it seeks to reduce the embrace to the object of its pleasure, to what is in front of it. And so it throws out its arms – according to the image from the *Aeneid* – and grasps nothing. It embraces and grasps nothing.[24]

Therefore, after faith, freedom: faith becomes the source of affectivity, that is, of an energy of adherence to being, to what exists, to reality in its totality.

Obedience

The dynamism of freedom doesn't know the road to adhere to faith. It knows where it has to go, but it doesn't know how to get there.

Therefore, the Mystery, the object of faith, that man who speaks to John and Andrew, who knows where He comes from ("Listen to what He says, He says things that no one ever said!"), He Himself, He tells you what you have to do. He is the one who tells you how you must do it. He tells you through the companionship in which He places you. He tells you through His companionship in the place where He puts you, as Ratzinger says. Do you remember the 1996 Easter poster? "Faith is an obedience of heart to that form of teaching to which we have been entrusted."[25] "Obedience of heart" means friendship, because friendship is the supreme obedience. You cannot be friends with a person to whom you cannot be obedient. Because eventually, it will run you into the ground.

So "faith, freedom and obedience," or "faith, freedom and friendship." It is very important to understand the demarcation between obedience and friendship. If obedience shows you what you have to follow to reach your destiny, what is friendship? It's a companionship guided to destiny. Guided – in other words, you must obey.

This is visible in an incredible way in the Movement and in *Memores Domini*. They are all communities or companionships, yet how dissimilar they can be! What distinguishes them is the strength of the obedience that they live, and the strength of the obedience they live stabilizes the strength of the friendship that exists among them. If they live the unity of obedience, they will certainly be closer friends among themselves. If, instead, each one follows what he or she thinks, is free to follow what he or she thinks, each will be divided from the other. Not even two of them will be united, not even if they get married!

Therefore, this trio of words – faith, freedom, and obedience or friendship – represents the trio of the fundamental words of all our living: justice is faith, freedom is faith, and love is faith that is translated into the concreteness of a companionship. These three words determine what you are and will be. To confuse these words or to lack clarity about these words means to lose your orientation.

Thus, a house isn't wonderful because everyone is friends, inasmuch as they are lively and content. You need to see *why* they are that way! It is the "why they are like that" that renders their living together stable and not mendacious. It becomes, in fact, a sharing of destiny, sharing the path to destiny.

This is interesting. When a house is made up of people who are good friends among themselves because they really, consciously share destiny, everyone in a house like this – to the degree that they participate – if they find themselves alone, they are able to create a community wherever they are. Because no one is alone. Jesus said that. No one is alone, not because one senses that one's together with who knows who, with God, or with Christ. To feel that you are together with God and with Christ means to sense that you are together with the people with whom He has placed you!

I'll repeat this very beautiful observation: in the companionship in which He placed us, we walk toward Him guided and therefore secure – and this means starting from the attraction we humanly have for individual people. What naturally attracts is empowered. It's assured, and it bears fruit. Otherwise, what naturally attracts us stops us, it would stop us. Did you understand? This is the most important thing.

Christ calls us within a companionship through which we are guided to go to Him – and this is the great surety, faith. It's the great certainty, the great faith – in which we are truly free, because we adhere to something that attracts us. In the companionship in which Christ puts us, all the force of attraction that the individual factors exercise on us remains intact. Nothing that attracts us is denied. You begin from what attracts you. This is freedom. Otherwise, what attracts us stops us. Instead of bringing us to our destiny, it stops us. Nine hundred and ninety-nine out of a thousand people in the world act like this. They follow and adhere to what attracts them because it attracts them, as it attracts them in the present, in the circumstances that present themselves. After a while, they're suffocated, and they can't *not* admit division as a fundamental principle of living together.

The problem of the indissolubility of marriage is the great sign of any human companionship: it can't last. If it lasts, it's due to interest in political or economic power, because satisfaction as such is so flimsy that it immediately decays. It seems that it's not decaying until the moment you get it; once you have it, it decays. Therefore, what do you do to have something through which God is attracting us – without it decaying? The more the presence of the other awakens the passion for his or her destiny in you; that is, it truly becomes love. Friendship, which is mutual love, is the law of obedience.

Season these ingredients as you wish (make minestrone, pasta ...) but if you leave these elements out, nothing you make will be edible, nothing will be palatable. You'll eat, but it will sit in your stomach and no Alka-Seltzer is going to help you!

Notes

CHAPTER 1

1 See Luigi Giussani, *The Religious Sense* (Montreal: McGill-Queen's University Press 1997), 16–17.

2 See Giussani, *The Religious Sense*, 116–19.

3 See Giussani, *The Religious Sense*, 27.

4 The official order of daily prayer in the Church.

5 See Psalm 118.

6 See Giussani, *The Religious Sense*, 23–33.

7 See Luigi Giussani, *At the Origin of the Christian Claim* (Montreal: McGill-Queen's University Press 1998), 43–8.

8 See John 1:35 ff.

9 See Giussani, *At the Origin of the Christian Claim*, 49–58.

10 Giussani, *The Religious Sense,* 7–9.

11 Thomas à Kempis, *Imitation of Christ.* Leo Sherley-Price, trans. (Middlesex, UK: Penguin Books 1952), 58.

12 Giussani, *At the Origin of the Christian Claim,* 59–65.

13 Giovanni Pascoli, "The Kite." June Osborne, trans. In June Osborne, *Urbino: The Story of a Renaissance City* (London: Frances Lincoln Ltd 2003), 188–91.

14 Editor's note: Giacomo Leopardi (1798–1837) is considered to be one of Italy's greatest poets.

15 See Matthew 16:26.

16 See Colossians 1:17.

17 See Matthew 28:20.

18 See Mark 9:14–28.

19 Matthew 11:25–6.

CHAPTER 2

1 John 11:45–6.

2 See Luigi Giussani, *The Religious Sense* (Montreal: McGill-Queen's University Press 1997), 29–30.

3 Luke 21:34–6.

4 See Giussani, *The Religious Sense*, 87–93.

5 Luigi Giussani, *Il senso di Dio e l'uomo moderno* (Milan: Rizzoli 1994), 65.

6 Dante Alighieri, *Purgatorio*, xvii. Dorothy L. Sayers, trans. (Harmondsworth: Penguin 1955), 127–9.

7 "Lost good: / a brief rocket in fallen tears. / What I grasped most covetously in my clenched fist came apart like the rose under the vault of eternity ... the more so for what I most treasured. / Everything paled, and was quiet, / lost colour and flavour, / (all the more for those things I liked more). / But, rigid with fear / of picking up again the gift that doesn't last, / I renounced happiness. / But a happiness / yet I can still ask of you, Lord, / one who looked / You for the elect of Your love: / that one – yes – to sing among the martyrs." O. Mazzoni, *We Sinners: Lyrics 1883–1936* (Bologna: Zanichelli 1930), 72.

8 See Matthew 11:25.

9 1 Timothy 4:4.

10 Matthew 10:30.

11 Matthew 18:6.

12 As can be observed in the diagram, no "segment" that man runs into is as wide as the angle that expresses his desire.

13 Saint Thomas Aquinas writes: Man's life consists in the affection that principally sustains him and in which he finds his greatest satisfaction." In *Un avvenimento di vita, cioè una storia: Itinerario di quindiei anni concepiti e vissuti* (Rome: EDIT Il Sabato 1993), 408. Cf. Thomas Aquinas, *Summa Theologiae*, II, II^ae, q. 179, a 1, *Respondeo*: "Unde etiam in hominibus vita uniuscuiusque hominis videtur esse id in quo maxime delectatur et cui maxime intendit."

14 2 Corinthians 5:16–17. Antiphon in the *Book of Hours* (Milan: Coop. Ed. Nuovo Mondo 1994), 114.

15 See Charles Moeller, *Sagesse Grecque et Paradoxe Chrétien* (Tournai-Paris: Casterman 1948), 17–29.

16 See Giussani, *Il senso di Dio e l'uomo moderno*, 93.

17 See Luke 22:42.

18 Vasily Grossman, *Life and Fate* (London: The Harvill Press 1985).

19 See Matthew 19:29; Mark 10:29–30.

20 G. Clericetti, *Clericettario* (Milan: Gribaudi 1993), 30. Editor's note: In the original Italian there is a play on the Italian words *righe* (lines) and *rughe* (wrinkles). The literal translation is "I can read between the wrinkles."

21 The bridge on the sea refers to the reflection of the Milky Way on the sea.

22 See Galatians 3:26–8; 2 Corinthians 5:17.

23 *The Unwritten Gospel: Ana and Agrapha of Jesus*. R. Dunkerley, ed. (London: Allen & Unwin 1925), 84.

24 Colossians 1:17.

25 See Psalms 115:5–6; 135:16–17.

26 Charles Peguy, *The Portico of the Mystery of the Second Virtue*. Dorothy Brown Aspinwall, trans. (Metuchen: Scarecrow Press 1970), 137.

27 2 Peter 3:9.

28 See John 5:17.

29 Genesis 3:19.

30 See 2 Thessalonians 3:10.

31 S.M. Giraud, *Prêtre et hostie – Notre-Seigneur Jésus-Christ et son prêtre considérés dans l'éminente dignité du sacerdoce et les saintes dispositions de l'état d'hostie* (Lyon and Paris: Delhomme & Briguet 1891).

32 Luigi Giussani, *Why the Church?* (Montreal: McGill-Queen's University Press 2001), 147.

33 "I did not know how to tell You how much I love You, God / in whom I believe, God who ar't life / living, and that already lived and that / to be lived beyond: beyond the confines / of the worlds, and where time doesn't exist. / I did not know: – but to You nothing hidden remains / of what is silent in the deep. Every act / of life, in me, was love. And I believed / whether for man, or work; or country / land, or those born from my solid roots, / or the flowers, the plants, the fruits that give sun / have substance, nutriment and light; / but it was love of You, who ar't in every thing / and creature present. And now / that one after the other have fallen by my side / the companions of my path, and more subdued / are the voices of the earth. Your / face beams with stronger splendor, / and Your voice is a song of glory. / Now – God whom I always loved – I love You knowing / that I love You; and the ineffable certainty / that everything was justice, even pain, / everything was good, even my evil, everything / for me You were and are makes me quiver / with a joy greater than death. / Abide with me, as night falls / on my house with mercy / of shadows and stars. That I hold out to You, at the table / humble, the poor little bread and pure water / of my poverty. Remain alone / beside me Your servant; and, in the silence / of beings, my heart hears only You." Ada Negri, "Atto d'amore." In *Il dono* (Milan: Mondadori 1936).

34 Giacomo Leopardi, "Nocturnal Song of a Nomadic Asian Shepherd." In *Giacomo Leopardi: Selected Prose and Poetry.* Iris Origo and John Heath-Stubbs, eds and trans. (London: Oxford University Press 1966), 277.

35 Dante, *Purgatorio*, iv, 114.

36 John 6:68.

37 See Giussani, *The Religious Sense*, 126–7.

38 Matthew 7:28–9.

39 John 7:46.

40 Charles Peguy, *The Mystery of the Holy Innocents*. Pansy Pakenham, trans. (London: The Harvill Press 1956), 100ff.

41 Genesis 1:26.

42 Giussani, *The Religious Sense*, 32.

CHAPTER 3

1 See Mark 6:30–44; John 6.

2 Matthew 9:36.

3 See Luigi Giussani, *The Religious Sense* (Montreal: McGill-Queen's University Press 1997), 7–9.

4 Philippians 2:5–11.

5 See John 17:1ff.

6 See the concepts of partial success and total success in L. Giussani, *Il Senso di Dio e l'Uomo Moderno* (Milan: Rizzoli 1994), 88–91.

7 See T.S. Eliot, *Choruses from "The Rock"* (London and Boston: Faber and Faber 1963), 176.

8 L. Giussani, *"The Journeying": He Is If He Changes* (Rome: 30 days 1994), 15.

9 See Philippians 2:8.

10 See John 4:8.

11 See Sirach 6:14.

12 Matthew 11:25.

13 Matthew 10:39.

14 Proverbs 21:28.

15 John 14:6.

16 "Shut your eyes, dear / that they not reflect the world / things are too near us / those things that we are not. // Only we must be, / the surrounding world has disappeared, / love reveals / all. – Shut your eyes." P. Lagerkvist, "Shut your Eyes." Trans. from the Italian in G. Oreglia, ed., *Poesie* (Forlì: Nuova Compagnia Editore 1991).

17 Quoted in D. Rondoni, "Un amicizia appassionata." *Tracce* 20:1 (Jan. 1994) 44–6.

18 Genesis 2:18.

19 See Psalms 113:9; 1 Samuel 2:5.

20 Genesis 12:2.

21 Luigi Giussani, "Un caffè in compagnia." In *Dalla fede un metodo* (Milan: Litterae Communionis-Tracce 1994), 27.

22 John 3:35.

23 A.S. Novaro, "Che dice la pioggerellina di marzo," verses 5–6. In *Il Cestello* (Milan: Mondadori 1910).

24 Virgil, *Aeneid,* vi. 700–3.

25 J. Ratzinger, from his talk at the presentation of the new *Catechism of the Catholic Church,* in *L'Osservatore Romano,* 20 January 1993.